The Mannerist Mind

An Architecture of Crisis

Francisco González de Canales

Table of Contents

Preface
Rafael Moneo

11   Nobody could have suspected, in 1527, with
Raphael's achievements still fresh —the merging
of antiquity and nature at the service of power to fulfil
the aesthetic mandate of the Renaissance, that an
event like il sacco di Roma would define and change the
course of history, triggering calls for a new worldview.
This tragedy was already foreshadowed by the Church's
waning authority in Europe and Italy's precarious political
situation, but artists were the first to see the need for
such change. They reacted by forsaking the desire for
balance and harmony, which had been so prominent in
Rome throughout the High Renaissance, to highlight,
instead, a reality dominated by uncertainty and unease in
the face of a world that was crumbling. Their works would
immediately reflect this situation, as they could not ignore
the turbulent atmosphere surrounding such events. Their
focus shifted in such a way that the artificial prevailed
over the natural, the cerebral over the instinctive, the
ambiguous over the obvious, the elaborate and elegant
over the spontaneous, the dark and the complex over the
clear and evident.

But if anything distinguishes the works from
that period is that —and this should be interpreted as a
paradox— far from abandoning the techniques the artists
had mastered and the iconographic content of their
works, they display an astonishing virtuosity and depth
of knowledge in the discipline that they practice. Artists
such as Giulio Romano, Parmigianino, Rosso Fiorentino,
Polidoro di Caravaggio, Bronzino, Pontormo —some
of whom were still close to Raphael, who himself may
have already suspected part of what was to come—
and, ultimately, Michelangelo (all names that critics and
historians agree on) show to what extent Mannerism —a
term that this period in the history of art is known by—
rests more on the subjective and the specific, that is, on

12   individuals, rather than on norms. And the attitude and principles shared by the artists who left Rome after il sacco, enriching the art in the cities they moved to, would have a definitive impact on the history of art, a fact that is underlined by the countless texts dedicated to the "arte di maniera" and Mannerism dating as far back as the seventeenth century. In his book, Francisco González de Canales provides a useful reminder of these texts, including those by Erwin Panofsky, Nicholas Pevsner, John Shearman, Craig Hugh Smyth and Wolfgang Lotz, without forgetting authors whose focus was mainly architecture, such as Colin Rowe and Manfredo Tafuri.

It is also important to mention that in FGC's opinion Mannerism should be understood not so much as a style, but as an artist's "mental attitude". This allows us to extend the qualifier to artists —and naturally architects— from other historical periods who may be perceived as related to it, to such an extent that their work is viewed as being dictated by the same principles. Hence it is appropriate to speak of the "mental attitude" to which FGC alludes. FGC thus agrees with Max Dvořák and Arnold Hauser, who believe that it makes sense to apply the Mannerism qualifier to artists, and naturally architects, from other historical periods provided that they interpret reality with the same attitude and principles as the artists from the sixteenth century that we call Mannerists.

It comes as no surprise that FGC refers to Robert Venturi and Denise Scott Brown as the architects who come the closest to Mannerism in recent history, especially if Venturi's early work is taken into consideration, such as his 1966 publication, Complexity and Contradiction in Architecture—more so than Learning from Las Vegas. The headings of the chapters in

13 Complexity and Contradiction, in fact, could be used as a means of listing the attributes that characterize Mannerist architects and the techniques they use. It is therefore only natural to find numerous examples drawn from the work of architects that are clearly Mannerist, and that for Venturi it makes sense to extend the term to other historical periods. We can see that FGC agrees with the validity of the "mental attitude" idea that is implicit in Venturi's text when he cites examples of works by such architects from the past as Vanbrugh, Hawksmoor, Fisher von Erlach, Furness and Lutyens, just to mention a few. And this [Mannerist] "mental attitude" can also be found in architects who are viewed as 'classic' figures of modern architecture. This is made evident by the fact that Sullivan, Wright, Le Corbusier, Moretti, Aalto, etc. are used as examples to argue his point, without forgetting that a figure as surprising and controversial as Armando Brassini is also included in this list.

On the other hand, the attention that Venturi pays to the figure of Louis Kahn, either by using his work as an example to support his opinions or by citing his writings as authoritative arguments to back them up, would serve as proof to confirm that Mannerism, as a "mental attitude", was still relevant during the second half of the twentieth century. In fact, we can clearly see that Venturi was aware of what his tastes were and of the fondness he felt for the principles promoted by the Mannerists in the way in which, after considering his first book as a "gentle manifesto", in 2000 he wrote a "new manifesto" with the title Viva Mannerism for an Architecture of Our Age.

While Robert Venturi used his own projects to illustrate his way of thinking and producing architecture, FGC has chosen to do so through the works of some

14   of his contemporaries, who he uses as examples
to underscore what he is illustrating. The works
that have been included in this publication have been
chosen to support a critical stance. Even though the
selected works refer to a wide range of circumstances
and programs, they all have something in common: they
share with early Roman Mannerist architects a respect
for what they know, something which may be described
as disciplinary knowledge. This respect is what brings
them all together, as it is what guides them all in their
professional practice. They are not committed to a style,
nor do they all use the same language or attempt to
anticipate the formal worlds to come. They simply make
use of the knowledge they have accumulated in what has
come to be known as architecture.

In these tumultuous times, how is it possible
to choose a handful of works by architects who adopt
this "mental attitude" that, according to FGC, inspired
the Mannerist architects? FGC dares to do so by offering
us, along with sharp and accurate commentaries, works
by Oliver Lütjens and Thomas Padmanabhan; Stephanie
McDonald and Tom Emerson; Kerten Geers and David
van Severen; Jan de Vydler, Inge Vinck and Jo Tailleu;
Jaume Mayol and Irene Pérez; María Charneco, Alfredo
Lérida, Guillermo López and Anna Puigjaner. If anything
enables us to see a relationship between these disparate
practices and their different works after their critical
reading by FGC, it is the fact that they all use their
knowledge of how architecture has evolved in the past
as a reference and a guide.

Realism supersedes utopia, with the
understanding that this is the best way to live in peace
with ourselves and the land we walk on, respecting the
legacy handed down by those who came before us.

15   FGC understands that all these professional practices share the same "mental attitude" as their peers, in which, "abandoning the naivety of perfect coherence, reflects the maturity of those who have faced the limitations of small commissions, doubtful clients, economic restrictions or complex starting conditions, and foster a special sensitivity towards what remains on the margins of architecture, always using the tools that architectural practice offers". Quite an audacity. Quite a manifesto.

Rafael Moneo, March 2023

Introduction 17

19   Human practices, which are acted upon the world as the result of a corpus of accumulated life experiences, advance through time driven by the continuity of their external conditions. Religious, political and social structures either enhance or challenge the conceptual and instrumental bases upon which these practices operate. These practices, however, inevitably conflict with established structures and conditions – every external inflection results in an arduous internal transformation. Today, for example, renewed ideas of ecology, gender, health and race are just some of the conditions that are unpicking our inherited practices and their subsequent consequences. It is urgent to address this shift in externalities in the most rigorous way possible to understand the resultant internal transformations that must take place.

   This book strives to situate this discussion not in the context of a specialized debate about these specific conditions (environmental, racial, gender and health issues…) but instead focuses on the deformations, deviations and questions

20 they produce in our field of work, that is, through the lens of the conceptual and material conflicts that are historically associated with the *mannerist attitude*. If we are to focus on practices themselves, then the debate around the practice of architecture includes a material question. Indeed, working with form – the act of giving material shape – is the most pressing question. This endeavor is not conceived merely from the perspective of architectural design, but reciprocally, from architecture as being inherently political. Any change to material that has been intended to be of consequence has a political question at its heart.

By focusing on the material, everyday and practice-related aspects of architecture we can determine a common body of experiences. It is from this common ground that we can recalibrate our professional response to the contemporary conditions within which we work and collectively construct a sustainable working practice. This collective construction includes a commitment to the transformation of knowledge as it exists

21 within everyday practice, a reassessment
    of our relationship with aesthetics
as a critical reserve and a continuous
questioning of the current systems that
architects implement to carry out their work.
These questions do not ignore the material,
mundane and practice-based realities
from which they emerged. A debate that
fails to address them could easily become
paralyzing, quietly diverting any substantive
change to the profession that we may
glimpse on the horizon.

22　What is 'mannerism'? Art critics from the seventeenth to the nineteenth centuries used the term pejoratively to represent everything affected, contrived or characterized by unnecessary gestures and excessive self-referentiality. Even though scholars like John Shearman or Wolfgang Lotz attempted to restore the term in the twentieth century to represent the extreme consciousness of elegant style, today it remains unusual to find it used without negative connotations. I would argue, however, that a new mannerist attitude is emerging in mainstream contemporary European architecture, appearing in the works of offices as varied and far afield as 6a architects in London, Amunt in Aachen, Baukuh in Milan, Office KGDVS in Brusssels, Lütjens Padmanabhan in Zurich, Monadnock in Rotterdam and De Vylder Vinck Taillieu in Gent.[1] This new approach engages with questions of the changing nature of the architectural discipline, awareness of context and craft. And it is these questions that form part of a discourse that has dominated the past

1　Even though these examples are representative of a specific generation that began their career in the twenty-first century, there already existed practices from a previous generation in which glimpses of a certain mannerist attitude could be identified. However, their stance was not hegemonic at the time, or at least not to begin with, and they were seen more like strong independent voices within the broader scene of the time. Just to point out a few, we could mention Valerio Olgiatti, Tomas de Paor, Arno Brandlhuber, the Barcelona-based duo Flores & Prats or the or the British firm Sergison Bates. The latter were closely related with the group that had formed around Tony Fretton. This group, which had been gathering at Fretton's house for over a decade, was formed by English architects with shared sensibilities and who, in a certain way, opposed the British status quo dominated by high tech architecture and by the digital neo avant-garde that leading figures such as Zaha Hadid represented. Stephen Bates, Jonathan Sergison, Adam Caruso, Peter St John, the critic Irenée Scalbert and, at one point, a young Tom Emerson (6a Architects) were part of this group.

23   decade.[2] Furthermore, there are observable affinities between these Europe-wide offices and those established in my own region of Spain throughout the beginning of twenty-first century, which includes Arquitectura-G in Barcelona, Anna & Eugeni Bach in Barcelona, Cuac Arquitectura in Granada, García-German Arquitectos in Madrid, H-Arquitectes in Barcelona, MAIO in Barcelona, TEd'A in Mallorca, Studio Wet in Seville and my own practice, Canales Lombardero in Seville.

This European generation of architects has grown out of a specific economic context. Due to a lack of public competitions and commissions, which were an important source of work and income up to the mid-2000s, our practices have grown, for the most part, thanks to private commissions. These have been mainly of a smaller scale and at a local level, which has developed a tendency for our practices to pursue architecture as craft. These types of commissions

---

2   For example, in this debate, a major role has been played by the review *San Rocco*, both by channeling interests and by identifying affinities. It was founded in Venice in 2010 and presented in the Biennale of that same year. Originally it was an initiative conceived by 2A+P/A, Stefano Graziani, pupilla grafik, Salottobuono, Giovanna Silva and the aforementioned Baukuh and Office KGDVS. It was edited by Matteo Ghidoni, while Matteo Costanzo, Francesca Pellicciari, Giovanni Piovene, Giovanna Silva and Pier Paolo Tamburelli (the latter from Baukuh) were part of its editorial board. The name of the review was taken from Aldo Rossi and Giorgio Grassi's well-known unbuilt project for Monza. The editorial in the first issue states: "San Rocco proposes the possibility of reusing architectural traditions that lie outside of private memory (contrary to Rossi's usual approach) without erasing personal contributions (contrary to Grassi's usual approach). In San Rocco, common does not mean dry, and personal does not mean egomaniacal. San Rocco seems to suggest the possibility of an architecture that is both open and personal, both monumental and fragile, both rational and questioning". Excerpt from "Editorial," *San Rocco 0* (summer 2010): 4. This continuous use of opposing concepts, of "both… and…", can be read as well as a clear reference to Venturi's intellectual world, something that would be one of the implicit interests of the magazine.

24   (extensions, renovations, single-family homes),
which have been considered conceptually inferior
traditionally, have led these practices to theoretically
frame the mundane realities and practical difficulties
that the profession has to address, such as budgetary
constraints, complex pre-existing conditions, the
ever-changing opinion of the client and the degree of
craftmanship needed to implement proposed design
solutions. In this sense, it has been all but inevitable
that these practices have abandoned the grandiose
architectural discourse employed by the previous
century's designers though competition entries, which
until very recently, defined the ethos of the profession.
Instead, I refer to a mannerism defined by "hands-on"
architecture, where architects have control over the
material and formal operations that they propose, all
within, paradoxically, the instability and complexity of
the mundane circumstances of practice today.

For today's architects, this first-hand
engagement with specific conditions does not come into
conflict with the intellectual vision and self-awareness
with which their architecture presents itself to the
world. For example, many architects take an inquisitive
stance towards the dissolution of the discipline and
the architectural object, both of which have been in
crisis for some time. It is precisely within this complex
set of circumstances that a mannerist attitude toward
architecture has evolved. Therefore, a conscious revision
of this term, and an interrogation of what it might mean

25 to be mannerist nowadays, is of utmost relevance.

This process of rediscovery can shed light not only on the work that contemporary practices are executing, but on their less-obvious affinities and precedents, allowing us to explore the deeper implications of their work also.

F_01

Part I

29 Mannerism had been effectively ostracized by the nineteenth century. The use of the term in contemporary architectural parlance remains pejorative, despite repeated attempts at its rescue throughout the twentieth century. In the 1920s, the German art historian Erwin Panofsky, known for his studies of iconography, played an important part in making mannerism conceptually relevant. In *Idea: A Concept in Art Theory* (1924), Panofsky approaches the artistic act in relation to the platonic notion of 'idea'.[3] This conceptual revision of art history, from antiquity to the classical period, is presented as a constant comparison between those artists "who know how to render only the sensory appearances of the material world," and others who, in contrast, "try to do justice to *idea* in their works".[4] According to Panofsky, while Renaissance theories propelled a return to naturalism, it was actually Mannerism which placed the *idea* at the center of its practice in order to reach *beauty*, not from the "simple sensory organs," but from a "spiritual interior sense".[5] This approach also allowed the historian to distance himself from traditional stylistic categorizations. In fact, for Panofsky, art had to be understood from the dominant "mental habit" that produces it and defines its idea of beauty.

This notion of "mental habit" or *Denkgewohnheit,* implicitly laid out in *Idea*, would reappear in Panofsky's later works.[6] Most importantly, however, from this new standpoint, mannerism can be considered a 'habit' or an 'attitude', which not only liberates the concept from the constraints of a closed stylistic category, but also releases it from its strict association to a specific timeframe within the Cinquecento. During

---

3   According *The Blackwell Dictionary of Western Philosophy*: "Plato used idea and eidos interchangeably for the non-sensible entities that are unchanging, eternal, and universal absolutes, the objects of knowledge, and the paradigms from which sensible things derive their reality. He held that these supreme entities are the essence or inner structure of things. (…) If you see with eyes, what you see is outer shape, but if you «see» with the soul –that is, think– what you get is essence or the common characteristic. Platonic ideas are objective, in contrast to ideas as subjective, mental ideas in modern philosophy", Nicholas Bunnin and Jiyuan Yu, *The Blackwell Dictionary of Western Philosophy* (Oxford: Blackwell publishing, 2004), 321.

4   Erwin Panofsky, *Idea. A Contribution to Art Theory* (Columbia: University of South Carolina Press, 1968), 3.

5   Panofsky, *Idea*, 89.

6   In them, Panofsky continues to dwell on the relationships between the ideological and philosophical universe of a time and its artistic production. One of his most important contributions in this sense is his work about the relationships between scholastic philosophy from the Middle Ages and the rise of Gothic architecture. As for the concept of "mental habit", see for example: Erwin Panofsky, *Gothic architecture and scholasticism* (New York: Meridian Books, 1957), 31 and ff.

the same years that Panofsky published *Idea*, the Austrian historian of Czech origin Max Dvořak, in his monumental work *Kunstgeschichte als Geistesgeschichte* (*The History of Art as the History of Ideas*, 1924), questioned the notion that mannerism was a concluded phenomenon. For Dvořak, Mannerism never really ended. Instead, it operated from the sixteenth century onward as a movement permeating the entire span of modernity.[7]

This appreciation becomes even clearer in the realm of written works. For a philologist like Ernst Robert Curtius, mannerism and classicism constantly clash throughout the history of literature, in such a way that mannerism is a recurrence regardless of periods and cannot be framed solely as a specific movement of the Cinquecento.[8] The diachronic interpretation of Mannerism that Curtis laid out was largely ignored when applied to other disciplines and creative fields such as architecture.[9] In this sense, the work of the German art historian Walter Friedlaender *Mannerism and Anti-Mannerism in Italian Painting* (1957) gave mannerism its own meaning and purpose within the visual arts, beyond being considered a deviant or derivative attitude within the works of the High Renaissance masters. For Friedlaender, the stylistic operations carried out by, until then, little known authors such as Rosso Fiorentino (1495-1540),

7   Max Dvořak, *Kunstgeschichte als Geistesgeschichte* (Munich: Piper, 1924), 270; cfr. Arnold Hauser, *Mannerism: the crisis of the Renaissance and the origin of Modern Art* (Cambridge, MA: Belknap Press of Harvard University Press, 1986), 16-17 (first published in 1965). Hauser adds on Dvořak: "Max Dvořak, who always refused to regard artistic styles as recurrent, did not regard Mannerism as an isolated historical phenomenon, but rather as a trend which has not ceased to exert influence since the sixteenth century". Hauser, *Mannerism*, 40.

8   Ernst Robert Curtius, *European literature and the Latin Middle Ages* (New York: Princeton University Press, 2013), 384-422. Curtius even went as far as to propose eliminating the term "baroque", given that in his such a category led to confusion. Panofsky does not include that term baroque in *Idea* either, as he goes from Mannerism to a new tendency that for him becomes prevalent in the seventeenth century: classicism.

9   There are some examples related to arts though. One of Curtius's disciples, Gustav Rene Hocke, applied the mannerism/classicism dialectic to the entirety of art history, therefore making the transhistorical vision of mannerism even more evident, albeit perhaps at times also more confusing. The group of artists to be considered by Hocke was you wide that could include Goya, Dalí or Picasso. Gustav René Hocke, *Die Welt als Labyrinth. Manier und Manie in der europäischen Kunst. Beiträge zur Ikonographie und Formgeschichte der europäischen Kunst von 1520 bis 1650 und der Gegenwart* (Hamburg: Rowohlt, 1957). I have accessed the Spanish version edited by Guadarrama from 1961, an English translation of this work does not exist.

31   Jacopo da Pontormo (1494-1557) or Parmigianino (1503-1540),[10] and the cross references established between them and other works and artistic practices, revealed the emergence of an implicit awareness of the autonomy of art as *artifice*. In the work of these authors, art manifests itself as circumscribed within a realm of references enclosed within its own cultural universe, therefore leading to its modern conception.[11] In this context, the rise in the Cinquecento of art history as a literary genre does not seem like a fortuitous event. Giorgio Vasari's *Lives of the Most Excellent Painters, Sculptors, and Architects* (1550 and 1568, in its extended version), is the first account of the practice of art not from a set of rules and unbreakable laws, but from the stance of the personal contributions that each artist provides from their own context and historical tradition, therefore showing an inevitable plurality in forms of making, or 'manieras', a term used by the Italian author. Vasari's volume is not the first dedicated to the biography of artists. However, by being the first to show art history as the result of the contribution of different individuals and their corresponding circumstances, the Italian author brings to the forefront the confrontation between the uniqueness of the genius and established rules, something that up until then the Renaissance had tried to avoid, or at least, pended addressing, as if this confrontation did not exist.[12]

It was during the 1960's that the reputation of the word 'mannerism' was first restored. At the 1961 Comité international d'histoire de l'art (CIHA) in New York, Mannerist art and architecture was addressed by a number of

---

10   Rosso Fiorentino and Jacopo da Pontorno were Florentine disciples of the master Andrea del Sarto, and their work *The descendance from the Cross* (Fiorentino in 1521 and Pontono in 1528) are excellent examples of the logic of mannerism in its most incipient state. In the same way Parmigianino, one of Corregio's disciples, with paintings such as his well-known *The Madonna with the Long Neck* (1535-1540), was also "discovered" by Friedlaender as one of the critical pioneers of Mannerism.

11   Walter Friedlaender, *Mannerism and Anti-Matterism in Italian Painting* (New York: Columbia University Press, 1957),3-46.

12   There are precedents such as *Liber de origine civitatis Florentiae et eiusdem famosis civibus,* by Filippo Villani or *La vita di Brunelleschi,* de Antoni di Tuccio Manetti. Vasari's work does not have the systematic presentation that Johann Joachim Winckelmann offers in *History of Art of the Antiquity,* which would inaugurate art history as we know it in the Modern era. However, Vasari's work does present, for the very first time, the history of art as the history of the contributions of different artists. For example, Vasari's obsession with Michelangelo as an artistic personality made it impossible for him to ignore the notion of the artistic genius. To consult the work of Vasari, a recommended source is translation, as it keeps more the flavour of the original Italian text. Giorgio Vasari, *The lives of the most excellent painters, sculptors, and architects* (New York: Modern Library, 2006).

figures including John Shearman, Craig Hugh Smyth and Wolfgang Lotz, all of whom would go on to publish more extensive books on the topic, including Lotz's historical text *Architecture in Italy 1500-1600*.[13] John Shearman published *Mannerism* in 1967, probably the clearest and best-structured reconsideration of both the term and as historical period. For Shearman, when addressing the historical reality of the time, *maniera* was widely understood as a positive attribute, when possessed by an artwork, or skillfulness and *savoir fair*, when related to an artist.[14] Being a fundamental contribution to the topic, *Mannerism* is the work of a classical art historian, able to date, classify and contextualize the works of a certain particular period, but not so much interested in looking into the philosophical, social and political consequences of this cultural experience.

The definitive work about Mannerism following this other line of inquiry is *Mannerism: The Crisis of the Renaissance and the Origin of Modern Art* (1965) by the Hungarian historian Arnold Hauser. The influence that Marxist thinkers such as Gyorgy Lukács had on Hauser explains why Hauser situated the work within the orbit of Critical Theory and why he posited that cultural constructions can only be mediated by the experience of the subject and its historical, economic, political and social context.[15] Fifty years after its publication, the book remains an authoritative work on Mannerism. Hauser released mannerism from its direct affiliation with the artistic movement of the same name and the terms most negative

13   I am referring to: Wolfgang Lotz, *Architecture in Italy, 1500-1600* (London: Penguin Books, 1974).

14   John Shearman, *Mannerism* (London: Penguin books, 1967), 16-17.

15   Critical theory was a line of thought founded during the first third of the twentieth century upon the postulates of neo-marxism. It proposes that knowledge cannot be objective, as the positivists of the time established, but that it was necessarily mediated by the experience of the subject, their historical, economic, political and social context. This theory grew around the Frankfurt School, with Walter Benjamin and Theodor Adorno standing out... I mention these two authors specifically because their work is especially relevant to the realm of culture (such as Benjamin's work about Paris or Adorno's work about the "regression of listening" in the music of his time). The critical approach of these authors strives to reveal the underlying ideology the produces a certain form of cultural or material expression—a critical stance that later on would also be taken by Manfredo Tafuri in his first works. It is important to point out that even though Gyorgy Lukacs is not a critical theorist strictly speaking, his works were precursors of it, and his thinking is considered critical to its theoretical approach. A recently publish introduction to critical thinking and the Frankfurt School can be found in: Stuart Jeffries, *Grand Hotel Abyss: The Lives of the Frankfurt School.* (London: Verso, 2016).

33 connotations—that which is deformed, over-acted and grotesque, and provides it with its individual meaning articulated by its own logic. This deep meaning is revealed through broad research into the economic, religious, and social issues that arise in the sixteenth century impacting all other realms of culture.[16] Therefore, for Hauser, Mannerism was not a poor cousin of the High Renaissance, but rather the very movement in which modern human experience emerged. The original movement conceived of a world based on the natural sciences, the flourishing of modern capitalism and the autonomy of politics. The reaction to these changes in the cultural production of the time will be reflected in diverse ways, ranging, for example, from the paradoxes presented in *Don Quixote* (1605-1615) by Miguel de Cervantes, to the rise of the genre of the *essais* as a form of critical-subjective writing in Michel de Montaigne.[17] Later, in the 1960s, the art historian Giulio Carlo Argan would conclude that "modern critique has rehabilitated battered mannerism" in his *Storia dell'arte italiana*.[18]

As the twentieth century progressed, this growing appreciation towards mannerism naturally permeated into architecture. As early as 1946, Nikolaus Pevsner dedicated *The Architecture of Mannerism* to 'the works he understood to be worth revisiting'.[19] Shortly after, in 1949, the historian Anthony Blunt caused a stir by praising the mannerist attitude in his talk "Mannerism in Architecture", given in the main hall at the Royal Institute of British Architects.[20] Therefore, it comes as no surprise that both Colin Rowe and Manfredo Tafuri, who at the beginning of the 1970s were very much leading architectural debate, dedicated time to the study of mannerism. In 1950, Rowe published "Mannerism and Modern Architecture" in the *Architectural Review*, one of the main international platforms of critical discussion in architecture. In this provocative article, the

16   Hauser, *Mannerism*, 3-61.
17   Hauser, 16-45.
18   A statement translated for this book from the original: "La critica moderna ha invece riabilitato il malfamato Manierismo" and Argan adds "un'arte indipendente dalla realtà oggettiva e mirante ad esprimere un'idea che l'artista ha in mente, è un'arte rivolta alla conoscenza del soggetto più che dell'oggetto e, quindi, assai più vicina alle concezioni estetiche moderne" Giulio Carlo Argan, *Storia dell'arte italiana II* (Florence: Sansoni, 1968), 7.
19   Nikolaus Pevsner, *The Architecture of Mannerism* (Londres: Routledge, 1946).
20   The talk was published in the insitution's review. Anthony Blunt, "Mannerism in Architecture," *Journal of the RIBA* 56, serie 3, no. 5 (1949): 195–201.

British theorist proposed a radically un-historical view of mannerism, pointing to some of Le Corbusier's works as contemporary models of that same "state of mind".[21]

Rowe bases this on a much-to-his-liking comparison between Palladio and Le Corbusier, one that had already appeared in "Mathematics of the Ideal Villa" (1947).[22] In this article, Rowe compares Palladio's and Le Corbusier's villas from a strictly formal point of view, using the now well-known diagrams of the iterations of the basic organizational elements of architecture (mainly walls and stairs) which Rudolf Wittkower produced from Palladio's villas.[23] For Rowe, Le Corbusier's villas were compositional variations of those same elements, which, despite the different history and ideology behind them, became, in Rowe's opinion, directly comparable.[24] In "Modernism and Modern Architecture", the comparison is made between Villa Schwob in La Chaux-de-Fonds (1916) by Le Corbusier and the Casa Cogollo in Vicenza (1572), which is attributed to Palladio. In both works, Rowe observes a mature working with a pre-established order. This interpretation avoided a singular stylistic way of interpreting these works, widening the perspective to include broader aesthetic values. In Casa Cogollo, the principal objective of the architect's brief was to renew the front of a house that originally had a chimney running up the façade. This unique problem led to a daring and novel solution, the use of a blank central panel across the front of the *piano nobile* itself, which to Rowe, is a brilliant and unexpected interpretation of classical language.[25] Rowe detects this same attitude in Le Corbusier's Villa Schwob, one of his earlier

21   In this sense, the "state of mind" is based on the idea, as Rowe recognizes of Panofsky's *"Denkgewohnheit,"* which in the theoretical case of architecture is taken to the last consequences. Colin Rowe, "Mannerism and Modern Architecture," *Architectural Review* 107 (March 1950): 289–299.

22   Colin Rowe, "Mathematics of the Ideal Villa: Palladio and Le Corbusier compared," *Architectural Review* 101 (March 1947): 101-4.

23   Published originally in Rudolf Wittkower, "Principle's of Palladio's Architecture," *Journal of the Warburg and Courtauld Institutes*, vol. 7 (1944): 102-122, and later, to a wider audience in Rudolf Wittkower, *Architectural Principles in the Age of Humanism* (London: The Warburg Institute, 1949).

24   Rowe, "Mathematics," 102. It is known that this discourse based on the pure rhetorical composition of basic elements of architecture (wall, columns, stair, patio) beyond all ideological considerations, is crucial to the beginning of Peter Eisenman's career, and that in part, his first houses from the 1960s are derived from this. And more recently, in an interesting essay, Pier Vittorio Aureli has identified Eisenman use of history and approach to practice also as mannerist. See Pier Vittorio Aureli, "Mannerism, or the «Manner» at the Time of Eisenman," in *Peter Eisenman. Barefoot on White-Hot Walls*, ed. Peter Noever (Vienna: Hatje Cantz, 2004), 66–74.

25   Rowe, "Mannerism," 290–291.

works. Here, the appearance of another blank panel covering a prominent area of the main façade is due to the need to adapt the composition to the placement of the staircase, leading to an unexpected variation within Le Corbusier's newly posited Dom-Ino system.[26] In a display of his own cerebral dandyism, Rowe defines mannerism as a form of intellectual superiority, or in his own words, "as an attitude of dissent," which for him "demands an orthodoxy within whose frame-work it might be heretical." [27] Rowe's position wasn't forgotten in the following decades, and two of his foremost followers, Peter Eisenman and James Stirling, would both be referred to at one stage or another in their careers as mannerist masters.[28]

F_02

F_03

26   Rowe, 292. The Dom-Ino was proposed a year earlier by Le Corbusier and used in this villa, as the images of its construction show published in Le Corbusier's *Complete Works*.

27   Rowe, 292.

28   I have referred to Aureli's attempt to define Eisenman as mannerist master in a previous note through his essay "Mannerism, or the «Manner» at the Time of Eisenman" (see note 24). The description of Stirling as a mannerist master can be found for instance in: Robert Maxwell, "Situating Stirling," *Architectural Review* 1370 (April 2011): 72-81.

Manfredo Tafuri also showed a great interest in the architecture of mannerism. Motivated by the discipline's sudden interest in the subject, Tafuri published *L'architettura del manierismo nel Cinquecento europeo* in 1966, though he would later claim the text as one of his lesser works.[29] However, some of his recurrent interests on the topic are already present, such as the emergence of the autonomy of reason, and its consequences to any practice in terms of reflectiveness and self-awareness.[30] After the publication of *L'architettura del manierismo nel Cinquecento europeo* most of the articles that followed related to this field of interest appeared mostly in minor publications, which were all fortunately abridged in the rather unknown *Retórica y experimentalismo (Rhetoric and Experimentalism*, 1978).[31] In contrast with Rowe, the Italian theorist addresses the issue by carrying out a study of Mannerism completely synchronous and contextualized withing the reality of the Cinquecento itself.[32] For Tafuri, one of the main characteristics of Mannerism is the rise of the self-critical consciousness within its authors.[33] In his words, in an artistic culture as energetically critical as mannerism "art, in fact, begins to see itself as a problem", in such a way that "a formal organization [might] wish to become self-critical investigations" and "there is an attempt to replace the process of giving shape by a critical process."[34] In this sense, for Tafuri, sixteenth-century Mannerism presented, for the first time, the

29   Andrew Leach has produced a well crafted introduction to this book in which he also explains his context, contribution, flaws and anticipation of Tafuri's better known works. According to Leach, Tafuri's own negative assessment of the book is present in an interview first published for the issue "Being Manfredo Tafuri" of *Architecture New York* in 1999. Andrew Leach, *Crisis on Crisis* (Basel: Standpunkte, 2017), 8.

30   Manfredo Tafuri, *L'architettura del manierismo nel Cinquecento europeo* (Rome: Officina de Architettura, 1966), 9.

31   Unfortunately only translated into Spanish, this work was published by the University of Seville after a series of classes Tafuri taught at the Escuela de Arquitectura de Sevilla in 1974, under the initiative of Víctor Pérez Escolano. This is the version of the text that I accessed here. Manfredo Tafuri, *Retórica y experimentalismo. Ensayos sobre la arquitectura de los siglos XVI y XVII* (Seville: Universidad de Sevilla, 1978).

32   Tafuri, *Retórica y experimentalismo,* 16-71.

33   Tafuri, 57.

34   Tafuri, 57.

same problematic that Modernism faced at the beginning of the twentieth century. This is, the simultaneous rise of an order and a counter-order, a break from naturalism, the proportional system and the general idea of harmony. This break was first expressed in the superimposition of compositions that were relatively severe and schematic, with organicist, overflowing and even irrational arrangements that Tafuri sees in the works of Michele Sanmicheli, Andres de Vandelvira, Pirro Ligoro or Giacomo della Porta. The epitome of this can be found in works such as the Teatro dell'acqua at Villa Aldobrandini, Frascati (1598-1602), by Carlo Maderno and Orazio Olivieri, where "nature" constantly reacts to the architecture, to such an extent that one of the main garden hedges acquires the height of what would be a superposed order. This could also be seen in the growing tensions between the rules of canonical orders and empirical-functional observations, as the expansion of the classical system could no longer conceal its confrontation —and at times even contradictions— with such mundane realities as construction, pre-existences, or program.[35] In short, for Tafuri, the mannerist self-critical conscience appears in correlation with the end of the univocal relationship between history and nature, the fall of humanist naturalism—something that, according to Tafuri, was a remnant of medieval theology – and the inevitable rise of awareness of a subjective dimension in all works.[36]

F_04

F_05

35   Tafuri, 59-66.
36   Tafuri, 33-36.

38   Beyond Rowe and Tafuri's stances, the architects who have contributed the most to the advancement of a mannerist attitude in architecture have been Robert Venturi and Denise Scott Brown. Framing our debate on architectural design and composition, I am referring more to Venturi's contribution to the notion in *Complexity and Contradiction in Architecture* (1965) than to the ideas he expressed in *Learning from Las Vegas* with Denise Scott Brown (1972), as in the former there is a lesser emphasis on the symbolic component of architecture, and instead the formal, (or even) material or building aspects take on a more prominent role. Venturi's interest in mannerism goes back to the early 1950s,[37] but this does not mean that Scott Brown had no influence over Venturi's widely celebrated first volume.[38] Ever since the moment they met as faculty at UPenn in 1960, Venturi found an intellectual partner in Scott Brown, someone with whom he could discuss his unique view regarding mannerist attitudes in the practice of architecture.[39] And this was so because, as mentioned, and unlike what was happening in the

37   Venturi's interest in mannerism was already present in his first study on Michelangelo's Campidoglio as part of his Master's Thesis at Princeton "Context in Architectural Composition", and was widely expanded during his two-year tenure at the American Academy in Rome (1954-1956), and his travels across Europe. The teaching of Theories of Architecture at UPenn in the early 1960s consolidated the ideas later appeared in the book. Venturi's first essay on the Campidoglio, first published in *The Architectural Review* 113 (1953), is recovered in the volume: Denise Scott Brown, and Robert Venturi, *A View from the Campidoglio: Selected Essays 1953-1984* (New York: Harper and Row, 1984), 3-6. An in-depth study into Venturi's years at the American Academy in Rome can be found in: Martino Stierli, "In the Academy's Garden: Robert Venturi, the Grand Tour and the Revision of Modern Architecture," *AA Files* 56 (2007): 42-56. A context for Venturi's teachings at UPenn can be revised in: Lee Ann Custer, "Teaching Complexity and Contradiction at the University of Pennsylvania, 1961-65," in *Complexity and Contradiction at Fifty*, Stierli, Martino and Brownlee, David B., eds. (New York: MOMA, 2019), 30-47.

38   Venturi was influenced by many colleagues at that time, which enabled him to process his intuitions regarding the idea of a mannerist attitude in architecture. In addition to Denise Scott Brown, another relevant influence is Kevin Roche, who Venturi met during his short stay at Eero Saarinen's office.

39   Venturi and Scott Brown taught consecutive semesters of the Theories course for architects from 1961 to 1963, which they had to coordinate together. According to Denise Scott Brown's own account in a recent conversation that I held with her, Venturi attended to most of Scott Brown's studio crits, and he was well aware of the innovative work and methodologies that she was developing. He also witnessed incremental housing proposals for her studios in contexts such as Soweto, Johannesburg, inspired by Edwin Lutyens schemes. According to Scott Brown's account, during those years they often had dinner together and had long talks about many different common interests. In 1964 she also joined Venturi's Theories seminar in their first joint academic collaboration. That same year they also worked together on the design competition for a Fountain in Philadelphia. Notes from a personal interview with Denise Scott Brown, on 15th of September of 2022.

39 US context, mannerism was an important topic of discussion in British academia around the time Scott Brown was completing her studies at the Architectural Association in London (1952-55).[40] The young South African architect was not only exposed to British pop artists, brutalism, "active socioplastics", self-help architectural schemes, and a new wave of social awareness in architecture and city planning. She was part of a circle in which mannerism was taken seriously for the first time in the recent history of architecture, and for two years she was taught directly by John Summerson at the AA, whose course on classicism at that time focused strongly on English and Italian mannerist architects. In addition, the intendedly provocative statement "is not Main Street almost all right?",[41] which appears in the last pages of *Complexity and Contradiction* is hard to understand without considering Scott Brown's influence.[42] This statement not only fully encapsulates the spirit of what *Learning from Las Vegas* is all about, but offers, with its "almost right" nature, an acceptance of the imperfections, of the contradictions and the conflicts that are at the heart of a mannerist attitude. Venturi and Scott Brown also referred jointly to a mannerist approach to architecture and planning in a much later publication: *Architecture as Signs and Systems: For a Mannerist Time* (2004). However, it is still in *Complexity and Contradiction* where the roots for a formal debate on mannerism can be better defined in their practice. It is worth noting that, in recent years, in the same way that *Learning from Las Vegas* received great attention from critics in the decades after its publication,[43] *Complexity*

40   She did Diploma at the Architectural Association from 1952 to 1954. One of the sixty-something students who graduated that same year at the AA was John F. C. Turner, who shortly afterwards became prominent in the development of self-help housing schemes by learning from the users' experiences of the context. After graduating, Scott Brown continued her studies for another semester starting in September 1954, as a post-graduate student at the new program of the AA Department of Tropical Studies. Initiated by Maxwell Fry and Jane Drew, with extensive experience in British Colonial West Africa and India, where they participated in the planning of Chandigarh, the course developed an interest in local surveys as a basis to design. Her first husband, Robert Scott Brown also joined this course. After a long trip to Italy, they decided to go to UPenn together, following Peter Smithson's advice to join Louis Kahn to complete a Master's degree in the US. These experiences reinforced the specific approach that Scott Brown began to develop in the first studio she taught at UPenn, with exercises in contexts such as South Africa.

41   Robert Venturi, *Complexity and Contradiction in Architecture* (New York: MoMA, 1965), 102.

42   Scott Brown's influence is more evident towards the end of the book, written when their relationship became closer.

43   Demonstrated in works such as: Aron Vinegar, and Michael J. Golec, eds.

40   *and Contradiction in Architecture* has continued to inspire subsequent publications and has been revised in two recent books of particular relevance: *The Difficult Whole*, by Kersten Geers, Jelena Pančevac and Andrea Zanderigo, and *Complexity and Contradiction at Fifty*, a collection of essays that celebrates the fiftieth anniversary of the original text at MoMA.[44] From page one, the original publication of *Complexity and Contradiction* seems to be an assertion of an intended mannerist attitude in architecture. The choice of Michelangelo's Porta Pia, built in Rome in 1561-65, as the cover image, was by no means unintentional.[45] In *Complexity and Contradiction*, Venturi calls for a return to the discipline and its specific knowledge set. This may seem like an obvious goal nowadays, but in the 1960s in the USA, at the height of the urban renewal movement, this was not as clear.[46] Therefore, in order to return to an awareness of so-called architectural knowledge, Venturi explores exemplary works, ranging from those of his own time to others dating from as far back as the Temple of Karnak, in Ancient Egypt. Porta Pia, in particular, is seen by Venturi as one of the masterpieces of historic Mannerism, with a composition of formal operations that is unique, which generates precisely the ambiguities and tensions that interested him the most. But

Relearning from Las Vegas (Minneapolis: University of Minnesota Press, 2009);
Hilar Stadler, and Martino Stierli, eds. *Las Vegas Studio – Images from the Archive of Robert Venturi and Denise Scott Brown* (Zurich: Scheidegger & Spiess, 2008);
Rem Koolhaas and Hans Ulrich Obrist, "Re-learning from Las Vegas. Interview with Denise Scott Brown and Robert Venturi," in *Content*, Rem Koolhaas, ed. (Cologne: Taschen, 2004), 150–157; or Enrique Walker's observations in *The ordinary*: Enrique Walker, *The Ordinary* (New York: Columbia University Press, 2018).

44   Kersten Geers, Jelena Pančevac, and Andrea Zanderigo, eds. *The Difficult Whole: A Reference Book on Robert Venturi, John Rauch and Denise Scott Brown* (Houston: Park Books, 2016). The analysis of the projects was carried out in collaboration with the students of the EPFL/ENAC in Lausanne. Martino Stierli, and David B. Brownlee, eds. *Complexity and Contradiction at Fifty* (New York: MOMA, 2019).

45   This image is found in the original book published by MoMA. Venturi, *Complexity*, cover.

46   It was Denise Scott Brown who developed the stance against the American *urban renewal* movement and specifically against the *crosstown* road network that traversed cities like New York, Boston or Philadelphia, something that Jane Jacobs had already denounced in her well known confrontations with Robert Moses. Scott Brown, who had developed an interest in what was known in the UK as "socioplastics", shared some of Jacobs' interests, to the point that she incorporated participatory measures in designs, such as in the interesting Plan for South Street in Philadelphia, which she oversaw for Venturi and Rauch from 1968 to 72. This work was commissioned by the grass-roots organization "Philadelfia Crosstwon Community" with the idea of showing alternatives to the introduction of the crossroads proposed by the administration, which would tear through the physical and social fabric of the city. See Denise Scott Brown, "An alternate proposal that builds on the character and population of South Street," *The Architectural Forum* 135, no. 3 (1971): 42-44.

41 Venturi's connection to mannerism is not a mere speculation. Indeed, the working title of *Complexity and Contradiction* was, almost until the final draft, *Mannerism in Architecture*.[47]

F_06

F_07

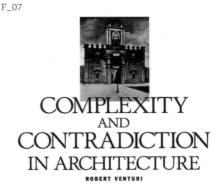

Moreover, his assertions of mannerism continued in later years, as his manifesto "Viva Mannerism for an Architecture for Our Age" for the 2000 Venice Biennale shows.[48] This manifesto can also be understood as a response to the works of the digital neo-avant-garde of the 1990s, of practices and architects such as Asymptote, Karl Chu, FOA, Mark Goulthorpe, Greg Lynn, Achim Menges, Reiser Umemoto, Patrick Schumacher, Lars Spuybroek and Massimiliano Fusksas, who was the curator of the Biennale. With "Viva Mannerism" Venturi confronts the break from the traditional discipline that these 'neo-avant-gardes' called for by researching into autonomous and self-sufficient formal generative systems. The manifesto can be understood as a continuation to his historical confrontation with the exuberant formal independence of Modernist organicism in the 1960s,

[47] For example, Emmanuel Petit declared that Venturi told him so in a personal interview in 2002. Emmanuel Petit, "Rowe, Scully, Venturi. Two Forms of Corbusianism," in *Complexity and Contradiction at Fifty*, 150.

[48] Published at a later date in the magazine *Log*, in Robert Venturi, "Viva Mannerism for an architecture for our age", *Log* 13 (2008): 52-53. The manifesto can also be found at https://biennalewiki.org/?p=3212. In 2004 he also published along with Denise Scott Brown Architecture as *Signs and Systems for a Mannerist Time* (Cambridge: Harvard University Press, 2004), situating the debate in urban terms.

exemplified in America by Paul Rudolph, and international-
ly by Jørn Utzon, as represented by his Sydney Opera House.
Rudolph, for instance, was used as a counterproposal in
Learning From Las Vegas.[49] Thirty-five years after *Complexity
and Contradiction in Architecture,* Venturi continued com-
mending the work of Michelangelo,[50] calling for an architecture which "didn't invent a new style, but adapted an existing
vocabulary and made it sublime", or as he later concludes, an
"Architecture that's in the end Mannerist, whose valid and
vital inconsistency creates aesthetic tension, and whose valid
and vital ambiguity enhances meaning: Viva Mannerism!"[51]
Therefore, after Dvořak or Curtius, the validity of mannerism has been a
recurrent theme throughout history, as shown in the growing interest in
the matter from the 1950s onwards, and the more recent recovery of this
legacy carried out by a diverse range of architects such as Kersten Geers
(Office KGDVS), Andrea Zanderigo (Baukuh) or Oliver Lütjens and Thomas
Padmanabhan (Lütjens Padmanabhan), among others.[52] What really binds
all of these diverse interests around mannerism? If we had to choose a
common denominator, this would probably be *crisis.* Hauser's book carries
this word in its title, hence, for Hauser, but also for Dvořak or Friedlaender,

49   Robert Venturi, Denise Scott Brown, and Steven Izenour, "The Duck and the
      decorated Shed", in *Learning from Las Vegas.* (Cambridge, MA: MIT Press, 1978),
      88-90.
50   As noted before, the first time Venturi shows an interest in Michelangelo is his
      study of the Campidoglio for his Master's thesis at Princeton, before his stay at
      the American Academy in Rome. Regarding this research, in 1953 he publishes the
      article: Robert Venturi, "The Campidoglio: A Case Study," *Architectural Review* 113,
      no. 32 (May 1953): 333–34.
51   Venturi, "Viva Mannerism," 53.
52   We have already mentioned the interest in this matter expressed by Kersten
      Geers founder of the practice OFFICE KGDVS in Brussels, in 2002 with David
      Van Severen, as seen in the book *The Difficult Whole* note 44), in which Andrea
      Zanderigo, co-founder of the practice Baukuh, founded in 2004 between Genoa-
      Milan also participated. Zanderigo is also one of the editors of San Rocco, which
      since 2010 has been a platform for the debate of these ideas. Lütjens Padmanabhan
      is a practice established by in Zurich, in 2007. Their interest in Mannerism can be
      seen in the course *Geometry order and Mannerism* they taught during the semester
      of Spring 2020 as guest professors at the la Harvard Graduate School of Design.
      They have also delved into Venturi's work in two articles for *San Rocco:* Thomas
      Padmanabhan, and Oliver Lütjens, "Venturi's First," *San Rocco* 4, (2010): 112- 115; "A
      day at the beach" in *San Rocco* 14 (2018): 206-209. The first is a reassessment of the
      North Penn Visiting Nurses' Association (Ambler, Pennsylvania, 1960-63), Venturi's
      first built work, with John Short, which is a crucial precedent for the Binningen II
      project of the Swiss duo. The second is dedicated to the Lieb house (Loveladies,
      New Jersey, 1967-69) by Venturi and Rauch, which is the built work that perhaps
      best depicts Venturi's interests in those first domestic projects from the 1960s.

the notion of crisis is at the center of a mannerist approach. "The fundamental mannerist feeling," Hauser points out, "is that there is no firm ground anywhere under one's feet" – and we will never have this again.[53] That is, what is relevant to mannerism is that crisis is not temporary, but it is a common condition. As Curtius points out: "what we have called classical periods of florescence are isolated peaks."[54] Therefore, the crisis is the norm, the everyday territory within which one has to carry out his or her work, because the periods of stability represented by the High Renaissance or High Modernism were just brief instances, anomalous exceptions within the history of artistic and cultural production. As the Italian semiologist Umberto Eco much later noted: "mannerism is born whenever it is discovered that the world has no fixed center."[55]

It was Reinhart Koselleck who went the furthest in the conceptualization of the term 'crisis' during the second half of the twentieth century. In his research, compiled in the chapter "Crisis" of his *Geschichtliche Grundbegriffe* (*Basic Concepts in History*, 1972), Koselleck begins by referring to the origin of the term in ancient Greece.[56] Deriving originally from κρισί (separation), a crisis is linked to a decisive moment in which one must choose between critical but incompatible alternatives, i.e. life and death, condemnation and salvation. However, in the Hellenistic world, and in the various traditions that followed, the term crisis was seen as a paradox because it is based upon the objective conditions that define it and the subjective criteria used to diagnose it. Likewise, a crisis simultaneously contains aspects that are both objective and subjective, that is, a crisis is both objective and subjective at the same time, or in other words, the object in which a crisis manifests itself also contains the subjective stance in the form of *critique*.[57] It is this self-critical awareness with regards to the conditions or systems in which one operates

53   Hauser, *Mannerism*, 52.

54   Curtius, *European literature*, 274.

55   Stefano Rosso, and Umberto Eco, "A correspondence on postmodernism", 1983. Cifr. Leach, *Crisis on Crisis*, 17.

56   Accessed here in: Melvin Richter, and Michaela W. Richter, "Translation of Reinhart Koselleck's «Krise», in Geschichtliche Grundbegriffe," *Journal of the History of Ideas* 67, no. 2 (April 2006): 343-356; translated from, Otto Brunner, Werner Konze, and Reinhart Koselleck, eds. *Geschichtliche Grundbegriffe: Historisches Lexikon zur politisch-sozialen Sprache in Deutschland,* 8 volumes (Stuttgart: Klett-Cotta, 1972-97)

57   Richter, 358-361.

44

that a crisis calls for what provides depth (and topicality) to the mannerist attitude, and helps distance mannerism from the pejorative associations the term is often burdened with.[58] The understanding of mannerism as an awareness of crisis is found not only in architecture or the plastic arts, but literature, which is frequently referenced in *Complexity and Contradiction in Architecture*. For Venturi, the values of mannerism that he appreciates can be found both in Shakespeare's ambiguities of meaning and in T.S. Eliot's theoretical essays.[59] Venturi also adopted the reflections generated by American *New Criticism*, a twentieth-century theoretical literary trend that proposed the idea of 'close reading,' which advocated an approach to texts that focused on ambiguity and their internal contradiction. However, as Hauser accurately states, the magnum opus of literary mannerism was *Don Quixote*, as it reflects the mannerist paradox at its very core.[60] First published in 1605, *Don Quixote of la Mancha* is to a large extent a critique of humanism as a form of culture that is transmitted through books, or as Peter Sloterdijk describes in *Rules for the Human Zoo*, that chain of "thick letters to friends" which generates a well-read brotherhood and defines a common territory.[61] The originality of Miguel de Cervante's critique was to show how a self-involved bookish culture rather than elevating knowledge can instead lead to absurdity, madness and even the greatest of foolish acts, as illustrated in the figure of Alonso Quijano, a man consumed by chivalric literature. Ironically, this questioning of bookish culture is carried out through a book, a tool that is part of the system. In this way, humanist culture is not negated, but faced with its own contradictions from within.

Mannerism's self-critical element, which operates from within the system to test and question it, as well as to reveal its own contradictions, has also been frequently identified with the call for what is known as *pensée complexe* (complex thought).[62] During the first years of his career, the Sephardic

---

58 This self-awarness is what Tafuri found also relevant about Mannerism.
59 Venturi, *Complexity*, 28.
60 Hauser, *Mannerism*, 319-323.
61 Peter Sloterdijk, "Rules for the Human Zoo: a response to the Letter on Humanism," *Environment and Planning D: Society and Space* 27 (2009): 12.
62 The notion of "complex thought" was defined by the philosopher Edgar Morin as the capacity to interconnect the different and multiple dimensions that make up reality. Instead of a reductive and totalizing way of thinking, Morin advocates for a reflective thought that is capable of relating said dimensions in a holistic and transdisciplinary way. Even though his well-known introduction to complex thought (*Introduction à la pensée complexe*. Paris: Seuil, 1990) has yet to be translated into English, a brief approach to his ideas can be found in: Edgard

philosopher Edgar Morin, one of the most important defenders of this form of thought, was focused on understanding the concept of crisis from the aforementioned perspective. In his article "Pour une crisologie" ("For a crisologie," 1976), Morin describes how, during the twentieth century, the notion of crisis has infiltrated every corner of contemporary conscience, made evident by conversations involving the crisis of capitalism, of work, of society, of family, etc.[63] However, instead of being drawn to more calamitous or apocalyptic definitions of the concept of crisis, Morin proposes its acceptance as a form of constant instability. In his opinion, this approach is a way of avoiding the conception of rigid and antiquated systems, instead, allowing for the development of complexity and flexibility. In his own words: "the richer the complexity, the more novel and unstable is the relationship between antagonism and complementariness, leading to more 'crisis' phenomena which, by transforming differences into oppositions, are disruptive and therefore, can bring about evolutionary reorganizations".[64] For Morin, the acceptance of the idea of crisis as permanent state leads to complex systems in which antagonist and complementary ideas are concomitant,[65] a notion which has its reflection in Venturi's simple formulation "both... and...". That is, instead of the reductive "either... or..." that can be identified in the discriminatory character of modern analytic thinking, "both... and..." is a form of complexity that, in Morin's view, is capable of responding to the constant instability of the present. Furthermore, Venturi's proposal was not the dissolution of the architectural object then in crisis, as most of the techno-utopian visions of the collectives of the 1960s and 70s—Archigram, Archzoom or Superstudio—called for. The positions of these groups were not only fiercely criticized by Rowe and Tafuri at the beginning of the 1970s,[66] but also by

Morin, "The Need for Complex Thought," *Sociétés* November. (1976): 149-163.

63   Edgard Morin, "Pour une crisologie," *Communications* 25 (1998): 57-62.
64   Morin, 152 (translated by the author).
65   Morin, 153.
66   Tafuri initially showed some sympathy towards these groups, but later his critique of them was shown in : Manfredo Tafuri, "Design and techno utopia" in Emilio Ambasz, ed. *Italy, the new domestic landscape: achievements and problems of Italian design* (New York: Museum of Modern Art, 1972), 388-404. Colin Rowe's

such unexpected figures as Rem Koolhaas. The latter, always a critical voice within the profession, pointed out that these groups had laid the groundwork for architecture's possible two main lines of defense: "dismantlement and disappearance". For Koolhaas, these two lines were both intellectually sound and factually inoperant, to the point of becoming sad metaphors of "pedantry" and ways of recovering the "former omnipotence" of architecture within the realm of the virtual in which perhaps "fascism may be pursued with impunity".[67] Instead of claiming the notions of dismantlement and disappearance, Venturi calls for maintaining the architectural object as a recognizable element which the subject must confront, while also manifesting that unstable condition, those tensions and ambiguities that are produced by dualities, adaptations and juxtapositions, something that in the last chapter of *Complexity and Contradiction* he defined as the responsibility towards a "difficult whole".[68]

It is of relevance to point out that in *Complexity and Contradiction* the principles of "both… and…" and "the difficult whole" are focused on the formal component of architecture, not on the symbolic aspect that is usually associated with Venturi, which would come later in his career. This formal component was seen for Venturi through the lens of Gestalt, a psychological approach born in Germany during the twentieth century prevalent in

critiques would appear in the catalogue for *Five Architects of New York,* and continued in the introduction of his book *Collage city.* Colin Rowe, "Introduction" in *Five Architects. Eisenman, Graves, Gwathmey, Hejduk, Meier* (Nueva York: Oxford University Press, 1975), 3-7. This text was previously published for the exhibition in 1972; Colin Rowe, and Fred Koetter, *Collage City* (Cambridge, MA: The MIT Press, 1978).

67   About "dismantlement" Koolhaas writes: "the world is decomposed into incompatible fractals of uniqueness, each a pretext for further disintegration of the whole: a paroxysm of fragmentation that turns the particular into a system. Behind this breakdown of program according to the smallest functional particles looms the perversely unconscious revenge of the old form- follows-function doctrine that drives the content of the project behind fireworks of intellectual and formal sophistication relentlessly toward the anticlimax of diagram, doubly disappointing since its aesthetic suggests the rich orchestration of chaos. In this landscape of dismemberment and phony disorder, each activity is put in its place". Meanwhile, regarding "disappearance" he writes: "Preempting architecture's actual disappearance, this avant-garde is experimenting with real or simulated virtuality, reclaiming, in the name of modesty, its former omnipotence in the world of virtual reality (where fascism may be pursued with impunity?)". Rem Koolhaas, "Bigness or the problem of Large Rem Koolhaas," in *Small, Medium, Large, Extra-Large* (New York: Monacelli Press, 1995), 506-508.

68   Venturi, *Complexity,* 89-133.

certain factions of art theory at the time.[69] For Venturi, the principles of Gestalt allow us to cognitively process form, that is, they establish the most basic categories to understand any form that is present to us. We ask questions like: 'is it one or two?,' 'are they superimposed?' or 'do they cross each other?' For him, these categories are critical to the way in which we approach any building: big/small, far/near, etc.[70] In fact, this is how *Complexity and Contradiction* actually begins: Are John Vanbrugh's front pavilions at Grimsthorpe Castle big or small, or are they far or near in relation to the building at the back? Is the Casa Il Girasole by Luigi Moretty on Via Piaroli in Rome (1949-50) a building with a central fissure or is it two buildings put together? Venturi's answer to these rhetorical questions is that what makes these buildings interesting is precisely this intentional ambiguity in their expression, the confusing character of their experience, the difficulty that we have processing them using the basic categories of recognition.[71] Additionally, Venturi's proposal cannot be understood as an anti-modern way of reasoning, to the contrary, he strives to elucidate a keener and more profound modernity, one without simplifications, something he finds, for example, in the poetry of T.S. Eliot.[72]

F_08

F_09

69   Perhaps the most influencing of these within the academic world of the US East Coast was developed by Kepes in *Language of vision*. Gyorgy Kepes, *Language of vision* (Chicago: Theobold, 1944).

70   Venturi, *Complexity*, 89-90. See also: Joan Ockman, "Robert Venturi and the idea of complexity in architecture circa 1966," in *Complexity and contradiction at fifty,* 81-84.

71   Venturi, *Complexity,* 28-29.

72   For Venturi, Eliot's critical writings are especially relevant, as well as how he advocates for a "difficult" poetry related with the diversity and complexity of his time. This is why the poet becomes ever more encompassing, more allusive and more indirect, all in order to force the language, distorting it just enough to turn it into new meaning. See: T. S. *Use of Poetry and Use of Criticism* (Harvard University Press. Cambridge, AM, 1933).

Moreover, the great mannerist he is, the examples that Venturi frames in *Complexity and Contradiction* are sourced from the full breadth of architectural history. Some have to do with the structure of space itself. The Church of Saint George in Bloomsbury by Nicholas Hawksmoor, in London (1720-1730) is one example of this. Due to the shape of the site and the urban layout, it is generated by two axes, the importance of which is contradictory: how must we read the main space? Longitudinally or transversally?[73] In other cases, the "difficult whole" has to do with the ability to introduce contingencies without dissolving the whole. In the Nobili-Tarugi Palazzo in Montepulciano (16th century), attributed to Antonio de Sangallo, a clear and repetitive order neutralizes the diverse sizes of the openings resulting from the program.[74] In the case of Louis Sullivan's Farmers and Merchants Bank in Columbus, Wisconsin (1919), the tension in the composition is underscored by the fact that the entrance is a superimposition of a door and a window (the result of solving the program).[75] Other resources can be used to introduce elements that are diverse and different to each other, as seen in Michelangelo's Porta Pia, where the layering of elements that are radically independent from each other is balanced thanks to the use of symmetry.

F_10

F_11

F_12
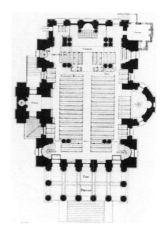

73   Venturi, *Complexity*, 34.
74   Venturi, 47.
75   Venturi, 90.

49 However, the most innovative tool that Venturi identifies as a unifier of diverse elements is what he calls "inflection" (taken from the critic Tristan Edwards).[76] This "inflection" can be understood as a trend, a twist or a general layout of the elements towards something. Venturi shows a clear example of this in the Birnau Church in Uhldingen-Muhlhofen (1747-50), by the Rococo architect Peter Thumb. Here, the features on either side of the central nave are different and non-symmetrical, but they all "inflect" towards the altar generating a tension between the many different elements and the inflection that unifies them.[77] Of all the manifestations suggested by "both… and…" perhaps Venturi's favorite is scalar ambiguity, which also provides a relevant urban dimension to architecture. This occurs for example in the Porta Pia, where the door appears to be constrained by the scale of the wall and clearly inscribed in it, while at the same time, contradictorily, a slender elevated element is placed above it providing the gate with a forceful urban scale. But this scalar ambiguity can be seen in other examples given by Venturi, such as Christ Church in Spitalfields by Sir Nicholas Hawksmoor, in London (1714-24), a building that contains three superimposed scales. The building is composed of three stacked elements that refer to different experiential scales. The pedestrian passing by hardly notices the spire at the top of this composition as the buttresses that flank the tower at the middle are so over-scaled. The decorative elements of the spire at the top operate at an urban scale, only visible as pedestrians approach from a distance. These superimposed architectural scales introduce a multi-dimensionality to the experience of this work.[78]

F_13

F_14

76   Arthur Trystan Edwards, *Architectura Style* (London: Faber and Gwyer, 1926). Cfr.
      Venturi, 91.
77   Venturi, 91.
78   Venturi, 36.

Venturi's first works, mainly minor projects in the Philadelphia area, clearly evidence these ideas. Take, for example, the unrealized Beach House (1959), the North Penn Visiting Nurses Association (1963) and the well-studied house for his mother in Chestnut Hill, Pennsylvania (1959-64). The Beach House juxtaposes two structures that are typical of American domestic architecture and merges them – two systems in tension. One composition is organized around a fireplace, a solid form, classical in nature and akin to the *federal style,* while the other composition features a terrace, conveying a sense of fluidity, with a grand window that opens on to the sea, an organic element that recalls the *shingle style.* Both approaches are taken to extremes: on one side of the building the inhabitant is made to enter through the fireplace, while on the other, he or she is provided with a vast, open and ambiguous space. These contrasting experiences are unified by diagonal layouts and inflections, generating that "difficult whole" that Venturi strived for.

At the North Penn Visiting Nurses Association, the scalar ambiguity that interests Venturi unfolds fully. On the one hand, the building aspires to convey a quasi-monumental nature when seen from a moving vehicle along the street. This is achieved by a series of unique formal manipulations, such as the introduction of a semibasement, thus creating a podium that elevates the upper fenestrated story, which, in turn, is deliberately stretched upward and lengthwise, extending the façade over the parking area to such an extent that a feeling of monumentality becomes inevitable. At the same time, the building presents a smaller scale, closer to that of the pedestrian and everyday life, which welcomes users as they approach the facility from the parking lot, a composition that is superimposed upon the previous scheme with the aim of creating a confusing sense of largeness and smallness at the same time. This scalar ambiguity is also expressed in its construction. The monumental windows on the main façade's upper level look like they have been carved into thick and robust loadbearing walls. Actually, these walls are made of CMUs[79], a humble, inexpensive and widely available material

---

79   In the USA, the term stands for cement masonry unit, and its use is widespread with both structural and non-structural purposes. It is a common material that can be found everywhere, from the crawl space foundations of suburban homes to the walls of American public schools.

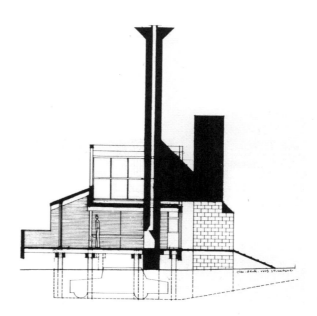

F_15

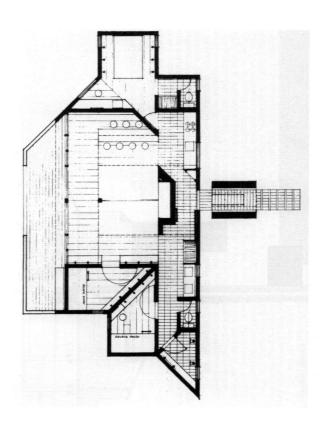

F_16

often associated with the most prosaic of architectures. The concavities that give the effect of this "fake thickness" are the result of formal manipulations that are not hidden, but somehow revealed by exposing the thinness of the panels cladding the window jambs expressing, therefore, the decorative nature of this depth. The monumentality of the window also conflicts with the structural possibilities of such a modestly constructed building. This is showcased by the need of a prop dividing it through the middle which somehow undermines this intended monumentality, albeit without totally effacing it. Inflection is also used as a tool; the organic excavation of the parking lot and the elevated angular geometry of the building, so different from one another, are "inflected" one over the other in order to create a whole.

F_17

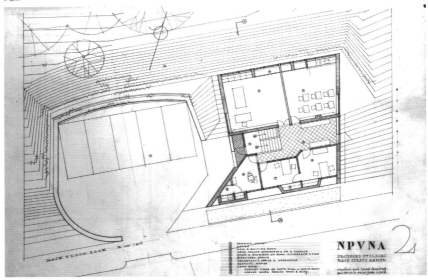

F_18

53

At the house for hir mother,[80] the scalar ambiguity seen at the North Penn Visiting Nurses Association is taken even further. Once again, the front façade monumentalizes American suburbia, and by extension, its inhabitant, with a proud and celebrated mother symbolically placed at the center of the iconic image of the house. In this case, the monumentalization of the house is achieved by means of a classical frontality that is almost ceremonial, referencing the arrival of a carriage to a grand villa, or in a more modern version, the approach of the car, as Le Corbuiser had experimented with at Villa Stein in Garches (1927). Meanwhile, this monumental scale coexists with another that is completely different and can only be appreciated from the side. This other scale, represented by that same mother sweeping the terrace, reveals the true modest and everyday character of the house. Both pictures were published in *Complexity and Contradiction* on page 118. However, over the course of the years, the second picture has not been referenced and reproduced as often as the first, despite the fact that, for Venturi, they necessarily complemented each other. Once again, the imposing frontal scale is the result of the layout of the program in section, with the inclusion of a small guest room, which, along with the elevation of the fireplace, produces a three-story façade for a house that only needs one storey.

F_19

F_20

80   Besides the writings dedicated to the house through the years of, among others, Vincent Scully, Stanislaus Von Moss or Rafael Moneo, its importance has led to a specific study of the evolution of its entire design. Schwartz, Frederic. Venturi, Robert and Rossi, Aldo: Mother's House. *The evolution of Vanna Venturi's House in Chesnut Hill.* (New York: Rizzoli, 1992.)

54 Compositional moves such as the entrance through the fireplace or the staircase at the house by the beach (two examples provided by Rowe) seem to repeat themselves in Venturi's house for his mother, as well as the inflection of the different parts of the house by means of diagonals towards the living room that unify a whole comprised of diverse parts. It should be noted that, beyond the aforementioned formal manipulations, in this house certain symbolic motifs coexist. The curved molding over the entrance into the dwelling forms a large arch signifying the entrance, while contrasting with the actual architectural construction of the linteled opening. The arch accentuates the clash between what is purely tectonic and what is symbolic communication. This device is also present at the North Penn Visiting Nurses Association, as well as at the Guild House in Philadelphia (1960-63) designed with Rauch, Cope and Lippincott, a project that interested Venturi in his early career. However, the explanations that he gives with regards to these projects in *Complexity and Contradiction* do not mention the communicative nature of this device, instead he focuses his reasoning on form.[81] Only in projects as explicitly symbolic as Grand's Restaurant in Philadelphia (1962), with John Short, or the competition for a fountain in Fairmount Park, also in Philadelphia (1964), with John Rauch and Denise Scott Brown, does he comment on the communicative element of the project. In this sense, Venturi prioritizes the formal aspect in the first theorization in *Complexity and Contradiction,* suggesting an approach through the principles of Gestalt. However, it is important to point out that this was not the only approach, as seen in the work of architects influenced by Venturi. This can be observed in works by Rafael Moneo, such as the extension of the headquarters for Bankinter (with Ramon Bescos, Madrid, 1972-76) where the juxtaposition of scales (with the fragmentation of the building into three different volumes) or the inflection of the entrance (with its unusual triangular shape seeking to face both the front and the side where preexisting building is located) reflect Venturi's formal explorations. However, Moneo uses these same tools to solve the way in which this extension project fits into its urban setting and responds to the preexisting buildings.[82]

81 Nevertheless, as early as 1965, and with some initial images of the house for Vanna Venturi which were still not final, Venturi would reflect upon this symbolic component in a brief essay that would contain relevant thoughts for what would be *Learning from Las Vegas,* written with Denise Scott. Robert Venturi, "A Justification for a Pop Architecture," *Arts and Architecture* 82, no. 4 (April 1965): 22.

82 A more in-depth look at the Bankinter project can be found in some of my previous

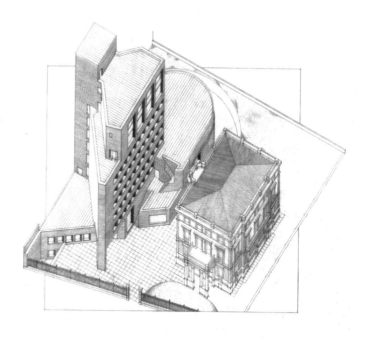

F_21

Likewise, Kersten Geers has identified aspects of Alvaro Siza's architecture that adopt some of Venturi's formal principles. However, in the case of Siza, these principles are utilized to solve the array of contingencies that he often tackles in his projects. In Geers's words: "Maybe we have to understand Siza as a better Venturi, one who found the energy to actually build the spatial ideas that were promised alongside the ducks and boxes, doing so in full awareness of these theories but without the necessity of reminding us of them. (…) Siza's buildings present the potential of Venturi's

writings, such as Francisco González de Canales, and Nicholas Ray, "Rafael Moneo and the search for a reflexive canon of knowledge," *The Journal of Architecture* 19, no.5 (2014): 693-722. In a private conversation with Moneo after presenting my report at the *Venturi y Nosotros* celebrated at the ETSAM (Architecture School of Madrid) in October 2019, he recognized the mannerism was deeply connected with knowledge, therefore understanding that this is a crucial factor in Venturi's interpretation.

work, when one forgets about the discussions connected to them".[83] In fact, Alvaro Siza himself has recognized, from time to time, Venturi's influence in his architecture, in projects such as the Banco Pinto & Sotto Mayor in Oliveira de Azemeis, a building that he defines as a radical acceptance of existing reality. Along these lines, Siza stated: "In my first works I would begin by observing the place, immediately following this with some classifications: this is good, I can appropriate such and such, this is horrible…. Nowadays I take everything into consideration, because what interests me is reality (…) In this sense we can talk about Venturi's influence. At the Banco in Oliveira de Azemeis, for example, multiple relationships exist between the building and everything that surrounds it. No classification is made between a 'good' architecture and a 'bad' architecture. Everything that exists is important, nothing can be excluded from reality. For me, Venturi's theories were very important; not only must we create relationships with reality, but also with spaces and materials. These relationships must be created between the project and its surroundings, but also, between the different parts of the project. Within the project, these relationships become tremendously eclectic and hybrid, since the realities that are external to the project can permeate and influence the entire design".[84]

F_22

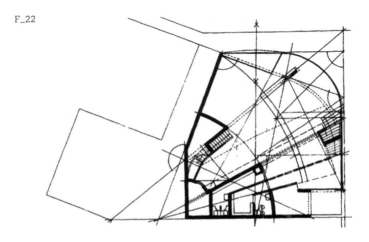

83   Kersten Geers "Siza's Mother," *San Rocco* 7 (2013): 19.
84   Christine Rousselot, and Laurent Beaudouin, "Entretien avec Alvaro Siza," *AMC* 44 (February, 1978): 36. Translated by the author.

Both in Venturi's work and in that of countless others who before and after him have adhered to the mannerist mental attitude, the formal or material operations that are carried out correspond to a constant questioning and awareness of the formal and material systems in which one has decided to design. In this sense, influenced by contingencies that are endlessly changing, these works can only be based on a permanent critical approach, reflecting the ambiguities, tensions and paradoxes that they themselves manifest. This context of relentless instability has been described for decades by authors from different backgrounds. Among them Anthony Giddens, the English sociologist known for *The Consequences of Modernity* (1990), Zygmunt Bauman, a Polish-British essayist and sociologist who produced *Liquid Modernity* (1999), Paolo Virno, an Italian neo-Marxist philosopher and philologist and a key figureheads of the post-workerism, who published *A Grammar for the multitude* (2001), and Frederick Jameson, the North American literary and cultural critic who published *A Singular Modernity* (2002). Beyond these lines of thought, the main characteristic of the mannerist stance is to openly and optimistically accept this crisis of permanent instability. Instead of discrediting all previous systems, and in the long term, undoing the possibility of creating any new system regardless of the inevitability of its tenuous validity, what the mannerist proposes is to embrace the critique of the system in which he or she decides to work. That is, to question the system from within taking it to the very limits of its possibilities and embracing its contradictions. Within this intellectual framework, it is no coincidence that a relevant corpus of the recent architecture that is produced nowadays in Europe seems to be touched by a certain 'mental attitude,' one which may well be aligned with a mannerist tradition in the way it addresses the present, from a position of self-critical awareness in the face of widespread conditions of uncertainty.

Part II

59

61 At the beginning of this book, mention is made of a group of European firms which are said to exhibit manifestations of what has been defined as a mannerist attitude. These include Lütjens Padmanabhan, 6a architects, Office Kersten Geers David Van Severen, architecten de vylder vinck taillieu, TEd'A and MAIO. It must be acknowledged that these firms have rarely explicitly aligned themselves with such a conceptualization. Perhaps only the Swiss duo of Oliver Lütjens and Thomas Padmanabhan, based in Zurich since 2007, has spoken directly and more than once about their interest in mannerism or the influence of Venturi, which in itself, in the Swiss context, could certainly be considered anathema. In a brief presentation, or manifesto, at the Schweizerisches Architekturmuseum (Swiss Architecture Museum) in Basel, they indicated their interest in "formal richness, densification, complexity and thoughtfulness" as the only way to work at a time when contexts have been highly impoverished.[85] Likewise, in one of their best-known projects to date, the small five-apartment building Binningen II, Zurich (2011-14), one can clearly notice continuous formal manipulations of the interests initiated by Venturi.[86] This includes, for example, the ambiguous scale of the building – even though it is a multi-family block, it fits comfortably within an area of single-family residences. This is a conscious decision, which serves to overcome the mismatch between the scale of the building on one hand (which would normally be dictated by program) and the urban context on the other, without having to diminish either of the two extremes of this equation. Indeed, this tension in the project produces a richness that reflects Lütjens Padmanabhan's particular aesthetic. Scalar ambiguity is not the only link to Venturi. Other likenesses include the articulation of the floor plan (which directly references the North Penn Visiting Nurses Association), the contradictions and ambiguities between structural elements, thresholds and partitions within the apartments, not to mention the painting pattern on the facade (so Venturian!) or the complex fenestration, which according to the architects themselves, refers to a solution by Michelangelo.[87]

85 This presentation is part of the Blind Dates initiative, organized in 2017 by the Schweizerisches ArchitekturMuseum in Basel. In its four sessions, this initiative has allowed emerging European offices to present their position through 5 minutes presentations. See: https://www.youtube.com/watch?v=RcgZRblO_Rk&t=101s, minute 1:57-2:05.

86 See for instance: Rob Wilson, "Fivefold," *Architectural Review* 1412 (October 2014): 56-69.

87 "We introduced a composite two-story window motif in which, in the manner of Michelangelo, a smaller window is suspended from an emphatically framed main

F_23

F_24

This very deliberate alignment with the mannerist tradition cannot always be ascribed to the other firms I have mentioned. In the case of 6a architects, a London-based firm run by Stephanie McDonald and Tom Emerson since 2001, there is an interest in the reflective, self-conscious traditions of the architectural discipline, as well as the inevitable conflicts involved in working with pre-existing structures, recovering the praxis of the 'as found'.[88] These interests not

window" http://www.luetjens-padmanabhan.ch/projects/binningen-ii (https://www.luetjens-padmanabhan.ch/projects/binningen-ii). Most probably, this refers to the solution adopted by the Italian master for the attic of Saint Peter at the Vatican. Michelangelo's fenestration at Saint Peter is also studied by Venturi in *Complexity and Contradiction*.

88   Term used by the architects Alison and Peter Smithson as a way of including given elements in their praxis. According to them: "In architecture, the «as found» aesthetic was something we thought we named in the early 1950s when we first

only manifest themselves through form, but also through accessible (almost sensual) craftsmanship, where matter is more than physical, considered a story-carrying agent — an attitude already evident in their seminal works like the Raven Row gallery (London, 2009).[89] The way 6a operates has been presented in the book *Never Modern* (by Irenée Scalbert and 6a) as a form of re-establishing relationships with premodern — if not primitive — sensibilities, linked to cognitive universes close to "the science of the concrete" and the figure of the *bricoleur* by the anthropologist Claude Lévi-Strauss.[90] Irenée Scalbert, a French critic based in London, also associates this way of ordering thought and working, which "goes back and forth between the intelligible and the sensible," with mythological figures like "Metis", defined in the book as a mixture of "flair, wisdom, forethought, subtlety of mind, deception, resourcefulness, vigilance, opportunism, varied skills, and experience".[91]

knew Nigel Henderson and saw in his photographs a perceptive recognition of the actuality around his house in Bethnal Green: children's pavement play-graphics; repetition of «kind» indoors used as site hoardings; the items in the detritus on bombed sites, such as the old boot, heaps of nails, fragments of sack or mesh and so on.' Setting ourselves the task of rethinking architecture in the early 1950s, we meant by the "as found" not only adjacent buildings but all those marks that constitute remembrancers in a place and that are to be read through finding out how the existing built fabric of the place had come to be as it was." Alison and Peter Smithson, "The «As Found» and the «Found,»" in David Robbins, ed. *The Independent Group: Postwar Britain and the Aesthetics of Plenty* (London and Cambridge, MA: The MIT Press, 1990), 201.

89   In Raven Row, a historical photograph of the building that the architects are transforming now into a gallery, with its rococo wooden ornaments completely burnt, opens the discourse on the use of charred timber. But it is also in the details, such as the handrails, that seem to keep the memory of the bodies that have used them, the memory of domesticity that is now lost.

90   I am referring to the so-called "science of the concrete" that Lévi-Strauss proposes in *The Savage Mind*. In "the science of the concrete", human language echoes the sensitive reconstruction of the world and the secondary meanings associated with sensations or phenomenological impressions. This establishes a more comprehensive relationship with the concrete, the immediate, the perceptible, and the everyday. The figure of the bricoleur, champion of the science of the concrete, defended by Lévi-Strauss in this book in contrast to the modern engineer, would be situated here from the ability of the mythical language to incorporate the sensitive and material properties of what it states, so that it allows us to establish relationships with the environment in which we live. Claude Lévi-Strauss, *The Savage Mind* (London: Weidenfeld and Nicolson, 1964), 1-34.

91   *Never Modern* is a book produced by the office together with London-based French architectural critic Irénée Scalbert. It is a beautifully crafted work, interesting as a cultural product in itself. Irénée Scalbert and 6a architects, *Never Modern* (Zurich: Park Books, 2013), 109.

Although the practice refuses to "advertise an explicit theoretical position",[92] and rejects any label or category for their work —and they would surely reject the mannerist label— a mannerist touch is easy to identify in many of their most celebrated projects, not least in the all-timber house extension in London known as the Tree House (2013), which in my view clearly locates 6a within the mannerist tradition.

F_25

F_26

I would like to dwell on this project to reinforce my argument. With the Tree House, the brief was to provide a new bedroom and ground-floor bathroom for a wheelchair user. At the same time, the gap between the north and south halves of the house, inherited from its origins as two small separate farmhouses built in the 1930s, had to be bridged. To develop this project, 6a revisited the traditional typology of the English gallery: a series of laterally connected rooms, amply illuminated and used as a space for *objets d'art*, mementos or artworks. The addition of a gallery to one's home has been a sign of opulence since the Tudor period and remains so even in modern examples like Team 4's Casa Creek Vean (Su

65   Brumwell, Wendy Cheesman, Norman Foster and Richard Rogers, Feock, 1966) and is even seen, with some aspiration, in more modest dwellings.

In the Tree House, 6a begins the formalization of the gallery in a canonical way, connecting spaces at the partition walls and taking advantage of the longitudinal orientation of the gallery to solve the existing level-difference between the front and back of the garden with a ramp, thereby also connecting it with the new bedroom. However, it is in the positioning of this new bedroom —at the point where the gallery turns and stretches deep into the garden— that a series of complex, ambiguous and contradictory relationships are generated. 6a usually explains the project from a pragmatic perspective: the important thing was to safeguard an existing tree, which in a way, now becomes the protagonist of the space. This way of working also makes them practitioners of that "other modern tradition" to which they are adjacent, and in which the English architects Alison and Peter Smithson are central figures.[93] For the Smithsons, the garden is not an abstract manifestation, as in many of the representations of Le Corbusier or Mies. The garden is a radically concrete, every day, situated experience, full of stories.[94] Instead of the generic trees seen in the ground plans of modern architects, which may or may not be real, for the Smithsons, "when we draw a tree, then there is a tree".[95] However, it should be noted that the aim of safeguarding the very real tree in the Tree House could have been achieved by many other means. In the 6a project, the extension of the gallery, which in reality has no purpose other than to house the new bedroom, is stretched and tensioned to the point that, more than an appendage or connection, it ends up occupying a length twice that of the existing house, thus completely transforming it by the

---

93   In Never Modern, Irénée Scalbert insistently refers to 6a's relationship with the legacy of Alison and Peter Smithson. Irénée Scalbert and 6a architects. Irénée Scalbert and 6a architects: Scalbert, 8, 12.

94   I have already referred extensively to the Smithsons' special relationship with the English garden tradition and their particular way of inhabiting it in: Francisco González de Canales, "A stay outside", in Experiments with life itself. (Barcelona and New York: Actar, 2012), 144-165.

95   Marco Vidotto, Alison + Peter Smithson. Works & Projects (Barcelona and New York: Whitney Library of Design and GG, 1997), 10.

addition of this one room. At the same time, the gallery as a connecting space, with its role as a busy service area, is set free and granted autonomy, thus generating a tension between its new independence and its continued role as a path of connection that remains an integral part of the house. The resulting gallery, of disproportionate scale in relation to the original house (or perhaps 'grotesque,' in the true mannerist sense?) is tamed by the inflection produced by the pre-existing tree, which adds a convex turn to its long trajectory. So, despite its disproportionate length, the extension becomes a sequence of encountered scenes that reduces the overall sense of scale and makes one focus on intimate areas, like the bookcase, the tree or the bedroom at the end. In this way, the gallery's relationships are reversed. Now the traditional glass enclosure becomes a self-absorbed space when the new extension, idiosyncratically made of old materials —reclaimed jarrah timbers in particular— begins with a controlled arrangement of discrete nooks that only look out to the immediate vicinity. It is only when you reach the very end of the gallery that you notice how it subtly turns around to look back at the original house. The paradoxical —and profoundly mannerist— aspect of this is that the gallery overlooks the garden along most of its length but within an architecture that seeks to rework the relationship between the house and the garden to create greater friction between them.

F_27

F_28

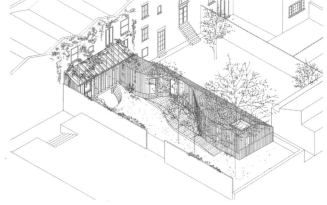

67 In the works of other firms, such as those of Office KGDVS in Brussels, directed since 2004 by Kerten Geers and David van Severen, we can also find traces of mannerism. An appreciation of Venturi's work is evident in the interesting reflections of Geers, together with Zanderigo and Pančevac, upon a rereading of the early works of the American architect based on its formal operations. For them, "Venturi's theory of practice turns the problems into tools through a process of *formalization*. Form is, to a certain extent, the materialization of a problem. (...) Venturi manages to distil the core of his own theory, the core of his project, from the very impossibility of resolving the issues surrounding the project. (...) Venturi's genius lays in his ability to bounce his main preoccupation back to his main occupation: he realizes he can only make a valid attempt to answer the enigma of the architectural Project by making architecture and by looking at architecture, by understanding architecture, by drawing architecture and by comparing architecture —fully aware of intentionality, its self-consciousness, against amateurism."[96] Speaking of his firm's own position, Geers states that "The architectural project thrives on radical ambiguity, where intentions are by definition conflicting and incomplete."[97] The critical self-consciousness that Geers finds in Venturi reflects a harmony with the mannerist ethos, but also the exploration of the project's irresolute nature and its inherent ambiguity, in a territory defined by disciplinary knowledge and the investigation of form in architecture. In this sense, Office's work has mainly been known for its intense formal concern, and specifically, for the form understood as perimeter or boundary separator. For Office, the form as a boundary discriminates between different conditions, environments and modes of being, beyond any programs or activities that may concern them. This formal discrimination is fundamental for them as a way to define and clarify one's own position as an inhabitant with respect to architecture as an artefact. They once stated that "We find it fascinating that over time the perimeters and the thresholds are precisely what survive. All the rest changes endlessly."[98] This limit or perimeter is not manifested literally, but as Juan Antonio Cortés has rightly pointed out, it is always constituted in the firm's work with a certain degree of ambiguity. The Spanish critic detects this approach right from their earliest projects, such as the Reception of

96   Kersten Geers, "The difficult whole" in *The Difficult Whole,* 17-18.
97   Geers, "Words Without Thoughts Never to Heaven Go," *2G* 63 (2012): 162.
98   Enrique Walker, "Kersten Geers and David Van Severen in conversation with Enrique Walker," *2 G* 63 (2012): 171.

68   Notaries Office in Antwerp (2002-03). Cortés refers to it in this way: "their intervention defines a new limit, in front of the existing walls, which generates an in-between space for lamps and storage and the entrance to the reception space from the public corridor and the passage leading to other rooms. A sense of ambiguity emerges in the materialization of this limit, a translucent mirror which perceptually dissolves into an infinite chain of effects of its translucent reflection".[99] Likewise, Office's formal exploration of the limit enjoys a certain autonomy with respect to its function, which is understood here as a contingency. This has led the firm to develop what they have termed "an architecture without content."[100] For the Belgian architects, "Architecture without content wants to investigate the possible architectural strategies left to us when we accept the limits of our field of operations".[101]

In this architecture, the metric, number and dimension also take on significance. The firm often presents its work as an ordered catalogue of variations of different formal operations on the same grid, which could well be equivalent to the rationalizing illustrations of the *Précis* by Durand, or more recently, to the modus operandi of the German architect Oswald Mathias Ungers, whose influence they have acknowledged.[102] From a formal point of view, one can't help but think of the matrix that the German historian Rudolf Wittkower used to compare the different formal compositions of the Palladian villas that became famous after the publication of his influential book *Architectural Principles in the Age of Humanism* (1949).[103] With Wittkower, the constant

99   Juan Antonio Cortés Vázquez de Parga, "Primary Actions. The Architecture of OFFICE," *El Croquis* 18 (2016): 23.

100   Geers has elaborated more on this notion in articles such as: Kersten Geers, "Architecture without Content," *Harvard design magazine* 43 (October 2016): 108-110. He also summarized his interest in this topic in a book developed together with students from different universities where he has been a visiting professor. Kersten Geers et al. *Architecture Without Content* (London: Bedford Press, 2015).

101   Kersten, "Words," 164.

102   There are numerous times in which this relationship has been made public. To place it in a close context, we could point out how they use it to reflect a distinction with respect to more immediate influences of their training, such as Ábalos & Herreros. Geers states: «Ábalos & Herreros drew ideas from the work of the Smithsons, Charles and Ray Eames, Mies and De la Sota. This work is also important for our own office. But our work has other influences, like Ungers and Rossi." Giovanna Borasi, dir. *AP164: Ábalos & Herreros. Selected by Kersten Geers and David Van Severen, Juan José Castellón González, Florian Idenburg and Jing Liu with an interpretation in photographs by Stefano Graziani* (Montreal: Canadian Centre for Architecture; Zurich: Park Books, 2016), 94.

103   Wittkower had already published this well-known matrix in the aforementioned

recurrence of "Palladianism" and its "neos-" is also evident.[104] It's of little surprise then that, to date, paradigmatic Office projects, such as the Villa in Buggenhout (2007-10), have often been identified as "Palladian."[105] This has led many to interpret the firm's work as a return to order that could lead to an understanding of its position as anti-mannerist. However, Tafuri himself pointed out that Palladio's architectural proposal was not so much the displacement of Mannerism as its logical conclusion.[106] For the Italian theorist, the Palladian project consists of reconstituting a kind of "new naturalism" to be understood paradoxically as a completely artificial articulated codex, established on the distance between the objective and the subject inherent to the scientific vision. In this way, architecture would be situated beyond any transcendental or eschatological hope held by the early humanists.[107] From this perspective, the most celebrated examples of Palladio's architecture, his villas, are realized projects, which unfold in the face of the crisis and social and economic reorganization taking place at that time in the Veneto. The Palladian villas act as articulators of these new relationships, both at the territorial level, as noted by Pier Vittorio Aureli,[108] and in terms of the organization of life itself. In this sense, the form is not stipulated

article "Principles of Palladio's Architecture" (1944), although it became truly influential with the publication of *Architectural Principles in the Age of Humanism* (1949), and especially, between post-war modern architects in the UK.

104 Thus, in England, to cite the most obvious example, the epochal Palladianism initiated by Inigo Jones at the beginning of the 17th century was followed by the so-called "neo-Palladianism" that Lord Burlington and his circle introduced as early as the 18th century. This did not consist of an already diminished replica of the Italian master, but rather gave rise to a period of special flourishing for English architecture with relevant productions by Colen Campbell, also the author of the influential Vitruvius Britannicus —who would propagate this ideal— but also by other talented architects such as the Adam brothers. It was precisely after the publication of Wittkower's book that an increasingly influential critic such as Reyner Banham spoke of a new Palladianism when referring to the Hunstanton school by Alison and Peter Smithson (1949-54). Furthermore, according to Banham, the impact of Wittkower's book was such that, among young British architects, "neo-Palladianism became the order of the day". Reyner Banham, "The new brutalism," *Architectural Review* 118 (December 1955): 358.

105 Cortés Vázquez de Parga, "Primary Actions," 30.

106 Tafuri, *Retórica y Experimentalismo*, 29.

107 Tafuri, 36 and 67.

108 Pier Vittorio Aureli, "Andrea Palladio and the project of an anti-ideal city," in *The Possibility of an Absolute Architecture* (New York: The MIT Press, 2011), 62-83.

as a representation of the natural, nor as an organic continuity with respect to the natural order, but as the point of reference from which reality can be made recognizable, encompassable and measurable, both at the territorial level, and in the dimensions of dwelling itself. For this reason, for Palladio, the architectural language of the room, as a principle from which the limits of habitation are established, is reduced to its most elementary manifestation. It is known, for example, that the Italian architect eschewed stonemasonry in the interiors of his villas. The expression of these rooms would no longer be fixed forever in stone, rather their modestly fabricated brick walls would be completed by the fluid and changing images that experienced painters like Paolo Veronese adorned them with. It is in this dialectic, between the informality of life and the reference that architecture sets as a limit, that we also must understand Office's position in relation to their architecture. Geers and van Severen understand "that order must be imposed, but only to allow life or disorder to reappear".[109] Following this approach, the floor plans for projects by Office are often organized as a matrix of *equipotential* rooms, in that they are the same size and shape, and therefore, have the same capacity for hosting activity or life. This matrix is offered as the means by which change and the different plans and activities, that is, the continuous contingencies of one's life, can be positioned. Thus, taken to the limit of its field of operations, architecture manifests itself as the paradox in which the imposition of strict regular order is the necessary precondition so that the most uncontrollable, the most subjective or even the wildest occurrences can take place.

This approach is developed not only in the Villa in Buggenhout, perhaps the most explicit in this sense, but also in other domestic projects such as the Villa in Linkebeek (2012-15), the Urban Villa in Brussels (2009-12) or the weekend house in Merchtem (2009-12). In these projects, the use of the enfilade as a union between the rooms is a recurring motif. As part of the exploration of the architecture of the threshold and the perimeter, these enfilades manifest a tense and ambiguous relationship between

109 Enrique Walker, "Kersten Geers and David Van Severen in conversation with Enrique Walker," *2G 63* (2012): 174.

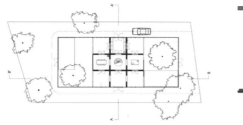

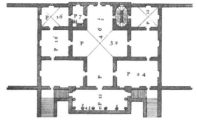

F_29   F_30

F_31

the limits that contain the room itself and the dissolution of them in the contiguous spaces that constitute the general matrix of the house. One project that perhaps takes these tensions and ambiguities further is the Urban Villa in Brussels (2009-12), a minor, local commission involving the expansion of a house on the edge of the small inner forest existing in Brussels. In this villa, instead of doing the obvious thing, which would be to extend the house towards the back garden, the project reworks a podium under the house, introducing a new order from which this pre-existing house is measured. This new order, defined by robust pillars, adapts to the existing wall structure, to which it must abut, and also manifests itself as an independent grid that develops an equipotential series of rooms crossed by a central corridor. It is the order imposed by the regular grid of pillars that provides a guideline for the possible appropriation of spaces. But in reality, it is a somewhat fictitious division of what can only be an open-plan hypostyle. This ambiguous display is reinforced by the way in which the glass enclosure is conceived, embedding its frames into the columns to increase their perception as free-standing objects. To achieve this effect, some of the columns are made in steel and cladded in wood to hide the functional window frame, thus avoiding the technical problems that embedding the glass into the concrete could have caused —as, for instance, Le Corbusier did in some projects such as La Tourette, the consequences of which we have all witnessed. Painted in grey, these cladded columns alternate with the concrete columns. This might be considered by some as a construction "deceit", but here the architects seem to think that the way in which architecture presents itself, its liberation from any clearly preconceived spatiality or form of inhabitation via an intended search for ambiguity, supersedes any moralistic rhetoric. The acceptance of this contradiction, to be able to deal with the mundane realities of the practice, such as complying with construction solutions that guarantee the comfortability of a house, it is not considered a limitation, or as an excuse to withdraw from intent, but as a possibility from which architecture itself finds its expression.

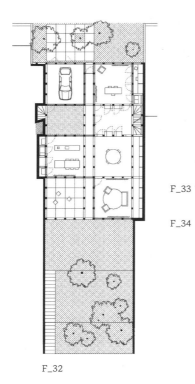

F_33

F_34

F_32

F_35

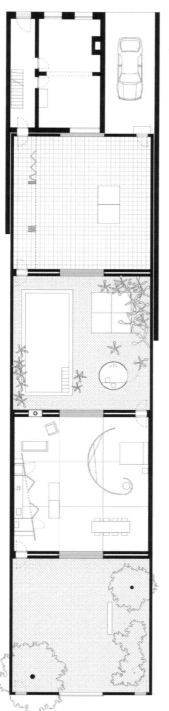

F_36

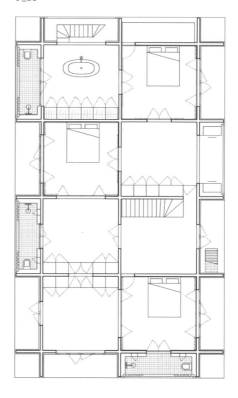

The tension between orders that, in principle are incompatible, is further pushed to the limit at Casa Solo, in Matarraña, Spain (2012-17). There is an insoluble tension in the house between open landscape and enclosed garden and courtyard, which is also formally expressed as the tension between a circumference that operates at the level of the roof as a reference to an elementary sense of cordoning off or closing a space, and the horizontal plane that inhabits the house as a square plateau expanded over the landscape.[110] In an attitude that we could understand as fundamentally mannerist, the project does not try to resolve this contradiction but rather manifest its consequences, as well as the possibilities that they offer to the living spaces. Casa Solo also exhibits another of Office's preoccupations, this time related to Venturi's idea of the "double functioning element".[111] This is manifested in its most intentional sense in certain elements generally considered to be strictly functional, like air conditioners, but which in Casa Solo are also incorporated with an expressive sense that punctuates the spatial relationships between the two planes within which the house unfolds. This machinery, usually banal, thus operates with a "double function" and its plastic properties not only condition the experience of the architecture, but initiate in themselves a process, perhaps still heretical today, of the subjectivation of the machine.[112]

---

110   A more complete description of this work can be found at: Kersten Geers David Van Severen, "Solo House, Matarraña (Teruel), 2012-2017," *Quaderns d'arquitectura i urbanisme* 270 (2018): 37-43.

111   For Venturi, the "double-functioning element" and the "both-and" are related, but there is a distinction: the "double-functioning element belongs more to the particulars of the use and the structure, while the "both-and" refers more to the relation of the part to the whole. This idea, which Venturi mainly relates to the building structure, could be considered more radical if it is extended to other building systems such as the installations. Venturi, *Complexity*, 38.

112   Office recognizes this incorporation perhaps as a legacy of their relationship with Ábalos & Herreros, as their Erasmus students at the ETSAM. See: Enrique Walker, "A conversation with Kersten Geers and David Van Severen," *El Croquis* 185 (2016), 16. I have already referred to the idea of "subjectifying the machine" in Francisco González de Canales, "Subjetivar la máquina. La casa Gordillo de Ábalos & Herreros," in *Arquitectura española y tecnología* (Sevilla: Recolectores Urbanos, 2020).

F_37

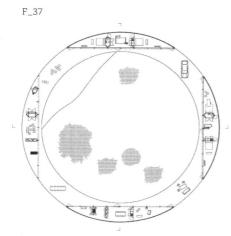

F_38

Apart from Office, the Belgian firm that can most explicitly be said to express a mannerist attitude — albeit from a very different sensitivity — is architecten de vylder vink taillieu (advvt). Indeed, some critics who have addressed their work have often characterized it as "mannerist".[113] Based in Ghent and officially founded by Jan de Vylder, Inge Vinck and Jo Tailleu in 2010.[114] the motto with which they often present the firm exaggerates Venturi's "both… and…" when they say their work is "about this and about that. And then so. And then this".[115] as if it is impossible to only have a single

113   See for instance: Christophe Van Gerrewey, "Ten opinions and misunderstandings about the work of architecten de vylder vinck taillieu," *2G* 66 (2013): 9; Carlos Quintans, "Optimism," *Archives* 3 (2018): 315.

114   The collaboration started in 2008. According to the description about the beginnings of the office that they offer on their website: "Initially the office started up in 2008 as «jan de vylder architecten bvba». Yet at that time Jan De Vylder and Inge Vinck were both principal architects. Before 2008 the office was called «jan de vylder en trice hofkens architecten fv», an office established by Jan De Vylder en Trice Hofkens in 2001. In 2008 Trice Hofkens quit the office. Until 2010 Jo Taillieu ran his own office under the name «jo taillieu architecten bvba»". See https://architectendvvt.com/about_us. Since spring 2019 Jo Taillieu, Inge Vinck and Jan De Vylder separated into architecten jan de vylder inge vinck and jo taillieu architecten.

115   Jan De Vylder, "So much. But what? About. About this and about that. And then so. And then this," in *architecten de vylder vinck taillieu: 1 boek 2* (Ghent: MER, 2011), 237.

focus, this being precisely the source of the rich aesthetic experience of their work.[116] The development of this sensitivity in the firm is undoubtedly linked to the context in which advvt work, often small private commissions for the extensions of houses, shops, refurbishment of buildings, etc., by clients who are not particularly interested in architecture. This has come about because in many of these projects, a certain interest is taken in the local vernacular of the Belgian peripheries, an anonymous architecture where professional architects have traditionally been uninvolved in construction, and has rarely been taken seriously by cultural or architectural critics.[117] Appreciation for the popular vernacular is part of an interest in context as a all-encompassing whole. It is not a question of an assessment of the place as a more- or less-regulated or cultured anthropological construction, but of "the whole context," from its most immediate and explicit form to its most vulnerable or absurd reality. It also includes the practicalities of the project, the architectural drawing, execution, and the clients, without the firm having to develop any theoretical position, although it is conscious and reflective, since the architectural theory is manifested in the physical construction. These architects have also rediscovered an immense enthusiasm for architecture and its broader links with the artistic and cultural world. In this sense, mannerism, as Rafael Moneo has indicated on occasion, above all, has to do with our conscious relationship with knowledge in our craft, and in this case, not only for this knowledge to be vindicated in practice but more broadly in its use, enjoyment, experience, in its link with one's own subjective life.[118] There is thus, despite the state of constant crisis —or perhaps, after finally accepting its inevitability— a certain optimism, a vitalist attitude towards knowledge that is not without a certain greed, which was also not alien to Venturi, Siza, Moneo, Eisenman or Stirling, and so many of the other architects mentioned in the book.

116   The office's catalogue of concerns, therefore, seems almost infinite, although when asked about how to define them with a little more precision, they have suggested lists such as the following: "About detail/ About timing/ About difference/ About production/ About context/ About references/ Also about uncertainty and the decisions./ And about what's unmistakable and the difference/ And about the strange and the normal/ And about the longing -poetry- and making sure things are different/ And about slowness and immediacy/ And about accuracy and gesture/ And about this moment and lasting much longer./ And about the unlikely -and even so!/ And about what will be won and what will be lost." architecten de vylder vinck taillieu, "Again," *2G* 66 (Barcelona: Gustavo Gili, 2013): 161.

117   There is no doubt that there are clear Venturian echoes in the development of this pop-vernacular sensibility.

118   This statement is formulated by Moneo during a conversation held after my first presentation on this topic in Madrid at the *Venturi and us* Congress, in Madrid, on October 28, 2019.

Much of the of the work taken on by advvt takes the form of small commissions, medium or modest dwellings that usually require extensions involving the opening up of space and aerating the tight architecture they have to work within. This opening up of the architecture, in conjunction with a particular appreciation for the existing condition, immediately produces dislocations or elements that seem to end up "out of place." In one of their first works, the Verzamel Werk Gallery (Ghent, 2001), the opening of the old kitchen to the living room leaves a suspended partition that still contains the space of the old doorway embedded in it, creating a particularly strange moment. In the subsequent Twiggy store (Ghent, 2012), the architecture also opens to accommodate the new layout required by the store. However, by not completely erasing what was there before, the modern store continues to bear the imprint of the old house. In this case, the removal of a slab, for example, leaves elements that were attached to the wall of the house suspended and dislocated, generating a disquieting sense of displacement. These playful contradictions, which leave previous elements of architecture as decontextualized *objet trouvé* create powerful images, and can be understood, perhaps, as a sympathy towards surrealism, a school of art for which there is no shortage of references in Belgium thanks to the provocative paintings of René Magritte.[119] There is also a deliberate tilt towards transgression in their work, resulting at times in buildings that *a priori* could be seen as sacrilegious in an architectural sense. In many of their lectures and reflections, advvt uses the image of a mural by Sol LeWitt in Ghent, which has had a banal intercom system built over it. The mural is an original by Lewitt, a remnant of the 1984 exhibition at the 't Gewad gallery, Centrum voor Actuele Kunst.

119   This relationship has been directly addressed by some critics such as Moritz Küng. In an essay for the monograph on the practice for *2G*, Küng makes an explicit comparison between moments in advvt projects and paintings by René Magritte. Moritz Küng, "Is there such a thing as Belgian Surrealism?," *2G* 66 (2013), 14-18. It is also interesting to note how the relationship with surrealism and the "object trouvé" has also appeared among critics when discussing works as different as those by 6a architects, when Irénée Scalbert, in this case, alludes to André Breton's "objective coincidence" as part of the bricoleur attitude of the office. Scalbert, 131.

When the gallery was turned into housing, the owner had the happy idea of placing the intercom system at the very center of the mural —although he had the deference not to eliminate it completely. This image, which would cause utter indignation in most people, is nevertheless like a *leit-motif* for the office, the necessary coincidence between the most banal and the most sublime —much to Venturi's taste, by the way— but taken here almost to the point of desecrating something sacred, or at least, something that could be considered sacred within a determined status quo.

F_39

F_40

Their insistence on working with the pre-existing leads advvt to find site-specific solutions to the challenges presented by the work site, rather than approaching projects with a totalizing logic. The Belgian critic Paul Vermeulen defines this way of doing things in the following way: "something that seemed no more than a clever invention, a flash of inspiration in the course of the work, the crafty elimination of a problem, gradually becomes the basis of an idea".[120] The end result, then, can look like a series of superimposed solutions, sometimes seen as layers of contradictory

120   Paul Vermeulen, "The Untamed Mind," in *architecten de vylder vinck taillieu,* 11. Note also that Vermeulen, like Scalbert and 6a, also echoes the figure of the bricoleur and *The Savage Mind* of Lévi-Strauss to explain the proceeding of advvt.

construction or structural systems: light wooden structures on thick concrete beams, heavy structures supported by thin metal elements, light metal beams on excessively heavy supports. Several of these systems can also appear simultaneously in the same project without an easily understandable order. In houses like Scheep Los (undisclosed place in Belgium, 2011), the particularity of each of these structural elements serves to punctuate the elongated continuous space created by the extension of the existing building. This is another way of understanding the "inflection" where the resounding continuity of the space is what allows, in this case, the appearance of a diversity of elements, thanks to which it maintains a general coherence. At the same time, it is this diversity of elements that attenuates the impact of the space, domesticating it and undermining any overwhelming, totalizing or coercive effect it could have on everyday life. It could be said that, in a tension that is not finally resolved, the feelings of spaciousness and breadth, and those of enclosure and confinement, coexist thanks to the deliberate ambiguity created by the architecture.

F_41

F_42

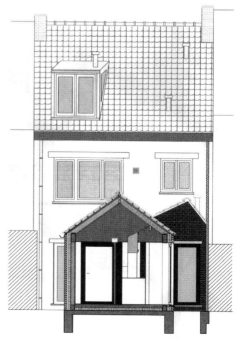

In advvt projects, it is often the typology, widely understood as a particular series of spatial relations, that gives consistency to the whole, while the material construction or the material interaction with the pre-existing structure continually calls it into question. In CG House (Undisclosed location in Belgium, 2016-17), the process starts from a kind of 'correction' of the existing building.[121] In this house, three independent agricultural constructions are constituted as a whole, as a single new house, with overlapping types 'correcting' the previous ones. This overlap between the two structures generates spatial richness, ambiguities and even, in the words of the architects themselves, "a certain degree of confusion".[122] This confusion stems from the inability to immediately understand the environment, the need to have to walk through it, observe it, relate to it in order to form some concept of it. In this sense, the necessary subjectivity —which seems to be always involved in the conceptualization of mannerism— is not only found in the architect as the maker, the subject who accepts the crisis in the systems in which they work, but also in the inhabitant who receives this architecture. The architecture is composed of everyday elements, yet the inhabitant cannot use their common, inherited codes to interpret the whole. They must reconstruct these codifications through their own experience. The disruption (or manipulation) of an existing code is both alien and recognizable at the same time. It thus becomes an architecture that needs to be discovered, that works with what is not easily classifiable, and whose ambiguity also makes it particularly resistant to an objective, measurable, numerical, "algorithmizable" coding, since its valorization is always translated through a non-transferable, subjective and personal sense of experience.

121   The term "correction" is common among many of the architects discussed in this book, as a way of measuring the project against certain contingencies. It is a term very frequently used by Office KGDVS to conceptualize some of their design operations. Their conversation with Enrique Walker 2G delves mainly into this idea of "correction" in his work. Enrique Walker, "Kersten Geers and David Van Severen in conversation," 170-175.

122   Jan de Vylder, "Constructing practice: architecten de vylder vinck taillieu," Lecture presented at Columbia GSAPP on the 2nd of March 2018. It can be watched online at: https://www.youtube.com/watch?v=ZQfhBOSecNo.

F_44

F_43

The ambiguity of architecture as a way of situating the experience is also very present in their other projects, especially with regard to the manipulation of the building enclosure. In this sense, they have followed an interesting route that perhaps began with House 43 (undisclosed place in Belgium, 2005). In this house, a sliding glass cover converts the space under it into a room that could be a living room or garden, or both at the same time. The incongruous composition of a glass cover overlapping a heavily tiled roof unleashes a series of exploratory paths in advvt's work relating to the boundaries of the enclosure. On a general level, the "dissolution of the room" has been one of the most recognizable avenues of formal and material research in the modern movement. Many architectural genealogies can be traced in relation to this notion of dissolution (Frank Lloyd Wright, Neoplasticist investigations, Constructivist experiments...) but one was to personify this tendency in a single figure, it would have to be Mies van der Rohe, with the Farnswoth House as the iconic example. Farnsworth not only offers the final dissolution of the perimeter, reduced to a thin vitreous film that seems to trap the diluted living environment, but the reconstitution of the room from the inside depending on the specific positioning of a central technological element (the core with bathroom/kitchen/fireplace) and the arrangement of the furniture. Furthermore, this method of organization is evident in the investigations of radical architecture that find their most obvious conceptualization and representation in Reyner Banham's so-called "bubble".[123] The continuation of these boundary-less architectures into the second half pf the 20th century made the "dissolution of the room" a relevant topic of discussion again in the 90s, advvt's formative period. This was especially true in Belgium where Stéphane Beel designed some extraordinarily sophisticated glass houses for that time.[124] advvt is so fond of using fine glass enclosures generated from materially-contradictory relationships that they can be jarring to look at. This is the case in the Rot-Ellen-Berg house (Oudenaarde, 2007-2011), an old inn that the owners inherited and wanted to convert into a house for their own use. In this project, the sturdy original brick house is kept as the envelope for an interior glass house, and opens up to a more diaphanous spatial division both in plan and section. While the glass house exists and shows its entire spatial opening, it does so within the pre-existing wall structure that isolates it, visually and thermally, and where ambiguous relationships between interior and exterior are continuously negotiated. All this tension seems to be balanced through the appearance of a massive ceramic fireplace, which remains as a stabilizing element around which the house revolves and which is also the only element that transgresses the house's two envelopes. In another of the firm's projects, the Production studios for Les Ballets C de

123   In the bubble the walls disappear and there is a displacement of the relationships "between" the inhabitants by a physically effective center. What Banham's bubble tries to show isn't simply a hyper-technological answer to modern inhabitation, but rather the placing in this way of all of the burden on the action of the inhabitants. In addition, in this domestic utopia there are no thresholds, and the door is literally left out. Inside and outside are in the same positive, transparent environment. François Dallegret drawing of this famous bubble appeared published in Banham's article "A home is not a house," *Art in America* 2 (1965): 70-79.

124   However, this frank and open liberation from the room has not always been received as liberation from domestic life. Architects who began to question the modern canon around the 60-the 70s, sought the liberation of everyday life from its opposite. The most representative and radical case is offered by the idea of architecture as a "mask" by the New York architect John Hejduk. Hejduk's mask is the first concealment, but then, at the same time, an expression of living. Perhaps this dual performance has to do with some pieces that Sol Lewitt made in the 70s, where he proceeded to erase, on photo plans of the cities, the places most commonly recognizable by people, and later, those where he had lived, the area of the city he had experienced, that is, that area of the city that he knew best and where he had lived, as shown in the work *Photo of Manhattan with the area between 117 Hester St., 420 W Broadway and Morty's Liquor Store cut out* (1979). For Hejduk, the house is based on the question of denying and occluding the room, of covering life to give to it its freedom and subjective expression. Hejduk's mask is an extension of the wall-house idea, where if the house hides the dwelling, the most transcendental event will be the moment of crossing into it, entering the veiled area. John Hejduk, *Mask of Medusa* (New York: Rizzoli, 1985). Edited by Kim Shkapich. See the chapter on the *wall houses*.

83 la B & LOD, Ghent (2003-2008), the ambiguity of the glass envelope is further taken to the extreme. Its relationship with the façade is in some way unclassifiable, as it passes interchangeably over open space, brick wall, concrete, stairs, metal structures... In this way, the glass is sometimes presented as a curtain wall, as a plating on the wall, or even as a window. The variety in the façade, and the different elements and materials that form it, appear almost indefinite in scale across the building, since each discrete element, column, beam, staircase, and brick wall seems to contain its own scale, apart from the general scale of the building that is never clearly perceived. As in previous cases, this results in the building being presented to us in an ambivalent way, showing itself to be both domestic and small, but also with strong infrastructural character.

F_46

F_45

F_47

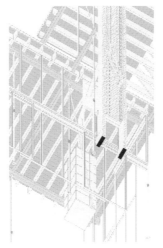

F_48

Finally, the exploration of the building enclosure is taken to its intentional limits in Caritas Jozef Karus (Melle, 2016), perhaps the firm's best-known work. This was an old psychiatric ward that couldn't be used because it contained asbestos and was due to be demolished to add a garden to the campus on which it was located. The proposal by advvt was to maintain the building but as a garden space rather than as a closed construction. Consequently, the partitions and envelopes of the original building were knocked down to free up space and generate new relationships while small, encapsulated environments were created within small greenhouses, which appear scattered between the pre-existing architecture. All the relationships between exterior and interior are distorted: the exterior lighting of streetlights enters the building, exterior garden elements such as greenhouses work like interior spaces, and trees grow inside the building. In reality, almost all the necessarily binary categories of architecture enter into crisis, not only 'inside' or 'outside,' but also 'acclimatized space' vs 'outdoor space,' 'permanent' vs 'ephemeral,' etc.

F_50

F_49

Apart from the architects mentioned above, attitudes towards project solutions that could be linked to theses traditions can also be found in the Spanish context. This can be said of TEd'A. Based in Palma de Mallorca, TEd'A arquitectes was founded in 2010 by architects Jaume Mayol and Irene Pérez, both of whom studied at the Escuela Técnica Superior de Arquitectura del Valles in Barcelona. Their work ranges from homes in Mallorca to international commissions like their School in Orsonnens, Switzerland (2013). TEd'A have always stressed their attraction to incorporating and revising their own traditions and approaching architecture as a craft rather than a profession. Thus, in the firm's own words, they "continue to perfect tradition as an indisputable heritage; defend regional identities against totalizing uniformism; prefer evolution to revolution; understand that architecture is lived from within and humanized from within by introducing space as the main theme; preferring corners, ambiguous spaces and spatial irregularities, understanding that architecture is nothing more than a support for life."[125]

> The firm has recognized not only the acceptance of contradictions in their work, but also perhaps the need for them on some deeper level. Jaume Mayol notes: "there's a contradiction inherent to the individual where, in the words of the singer JM Oliver, «I have a life that doesn't allow undo»... a contradiction that we must allow ourselves so as not to be driven mad by that «damned perfection»...but contradiction is also an inseparable part of coherence... the exception that proves the rule... why not? Turning it around, rethinking it, gambling, serious fun".[126]

For TEd'A, there is usually a certain formal and material system of organization. The most prevalent system is the logic of adjacent equipotential enclosures, defined by a heavily-walled structure, which guarantees optimal environmental performance in the hot Mediterranean climates in which most of their architecture is located. However, it seems as if in the subsequent development of the architecture, they emphasize a parenthesis or a continuous questioning of the system that they started with. This can be seen in Can Jaime i n'Isabelle, Palma de Mallorca (2011-18), a project dominated by a robust perimeter of equipotential patio/room

---

125   This text can be found at: https://www.upv.es/catedrablanca/CIAB6/ponentes/4teda/teda.htm.

126   Excerpted from an email received from Jaume Mayol as a response to a first draft of this text dating from April 2020.

enclosures that leaves, at its heart, and almost as a leftover, the silhouette of a complex courtyard that intermediates relationships while regulating the house's climate. However, this logic, which is clearly seen in the work models or the plan when cut at its upper level, seems to be blurred by the intense fragmentation of the experience of the house itself, capable of generating situations of indetermination and a diffuse understanding of the spatiality of the building —not to mention the continuous tension between system and element, lintels that are three-dimensional, structural components that seem to want to seek autonomy, and so many other elements that generate the ambiguities and tensions that form part of the practice's identity. This attitude to the project also generates a particular relationship with our experience of the house.

F_51

F_52

F_53

87

From a typological point of view, the house is built with a *courtyard-house* layout, whose centrality serves to order the way we relate to the various spaces. It is a stable reference, well-known within the long-standing social and material culture that sustains its use. However, the courtyard – which offers a kind of reassurance, a familiarity with its mechanisms, the daily practices we associate with it, and which gives us the reference points within which to situate our experiences – can also produce a heavy burden. Historically, its relational centrality has been implemented as a useful device for controlling family relationships, sometimes very explicitly. In traditional social settings, an important patriarchal figure (the grandfather, father or even the priest) would calmly take his natural place in the courtyard from where he would oversee all the domestic traffic, especially in the afternoons and on holidays, while getting some cooler, fresh air.[127] When the figure disappears, the patio-house apparatus, as in Foucault's panopticon, continues to perform its function.[128] Perhaps this is the problem with

[127] I have previously referred to this same question in "Politics of the domestic," in *José Ramón Sierra 2015* (Sevilla: Recolectores Urbanos), 78-105, where the patio is discussed as a device of domestic control reflected in culture i.e. in the plays by the Álvarez Quintero brothers. Some of these very popular plays from the first third of the 20th took place in the patio of the house as a stage. As indicated above, in the patio, family and social relationships unfold under the regulatory gaze of the patriarch of the family. In my childhood, I still remember that particular picture of the patio house, the one in which my grandparents lived in a town in Córdoba: my grandfather, his health already deteriorated, spent the entire day in the cool of the patio, with no other possible entertainment than observing from there the continuous flow of activities that occurred daily in the house. Any movement through it, and above all, any access to the house, always ran into his attentive gaze, sometimes accompanied by a fellow socialite, an older relative, or perhaps the priest.

[128] The Panopticon was devised at the end of the 18th century by the British philosopher and social reformer Jeremy Bentham. It was conceived as a circular prison typology with a security checkpoint in the center from which all the cells would be exposed. For Foucault, the panoptic is essential not so much for optimizing the number of guards needed to control the prison thanks to its geometry offering the guard a panoptic view, but because it is a control device that goes far beyond the presence of the guard. While the cells were constantly illuminated, the sentry box was always dark, so the inmate never knew for sure if a guard was watching them at that moment. In this way, the configuration of the panopticon guaranteed that the individual, whether there was a guard present or not, always had the feeling that someone was watching them, a sense that for Bentham should be internalized in the inmate as part of their re-education for social reintegration, so that once they were released, the feeling of being constantly watched would stay with them forever. Michel Foucault,

outright typological approaches in general, their inexora-
bility or strong predetermination towards certain lifestyles,
and their capacity for coercion. In Can Jaime i n'Isabelle, on
the contrary, the courtyard-house is affirmed but in turn, it
is dismantled, and in this dismantling, the capacity of the
courtyard is undermined as a control device by fragment-
ing it into various pockets of space, nooks and crannies and
small micro-ecosystems, to take shelter from any totalizing
gaze. The house is a courtyard-house, but it is at the same
time its opposite, an extensive inextricable garden, which
forces the inhabitant to get lost in it to understand it, dismantling any type of relationship or previous mental structure that we could have of this popular typology.

Another paradigmatic project that includes elements that could.be ascribed to a mannerist mindset is 110 Rooms by MAIO (Barcelona, 2013-
2106). Founded in Barcelona in 2006 and led by María Charneco,
Alfredo Lérida, Guillermo López and Anna Puigjaner, the firm began
by designing small-scale private commissions, which involved working

"Panopticism", in *Discipline & Punish: The Birth of the Prison.* (New York: Vintage Books, 1977), 195-228. A clarification on the notion of "apparatus" according to Michel Foucault can be found in Giorgio Agamben's conference *What is an apparatus?* (2005). For Agamben, some fundamental aspects define an apparatus: "a) It is a heterogeneous set that includes virtually anything, linguistic or non-linguistic, under the same heading: discourses, institutions, buildings, laws, police measures, philosophical propositions, and so on." As such, the device itself is the network that is established between these elements. "b) The apparatus always has a concrete strategic function and is always located in a power relation." In this sense, the apparatus is something general, a reseau, a «network» because it includes in itself the episteme, which is, for Foucault, that which in a given society allows us to distinguish what is accepted as a scientific statement from what is not scientific. "c) It appears at the intersection of power relations and relations of knowledge." Giorgio Agamben, "What is an apparatus?," in *What is an apparatus? And other essays* (Stanford, CA: Standford University Press, 2009), 2-3 Undoubtedly, the concept of biopower developed by Michel Foucault in a spatial genealogy that starts from the idea of the panopticon, is one of the most dominant ideas of this transition from space to practices, permeating both psychic states and unconscious and biological behaviors. That is why the apparatus that exercises this biopower does not only include the patio as a control diagram but also other more intangible means of re-education about what is and is not admissible for bourgeois society, and very clearly proliferated through Spanish theatre plays, paintings, songs and novels of the late 19th century and the first half of the 20th century that carried specific narratives linked to the patio. In Seville, for example, this is visible in the writings of illustrious Sevillians such as Joaquín Guichot, José Gestoso or Luis Montoto, the imaginary produced by Jiménez Aranda or Gonzalo Bilbao, the scenes of the Álvarez Quintero plays or the so-called "opera Flamenca" as the culmination of Sevillian folklore; that is to say, a whole socio-cultural discourse that would later be successfully collected by Sevillian regionalism.

F_54

F_55

F_56

with pre-existing structures like the renewal of a rural house in Manacor (Mallorca, 2008-2015), the Bar Nou (Barcelona, 2014-2015) and the transformation of a formal laundromat into their own office (Barcelona, 2011-12). In the 110 rooms extension in Barcelona, they take up a theme very familiar to Office KGDVS —the matrix of same-sized square rooms. Again, we find an equipotential floor plan, designed with versatile rooms. Here, the equivalence between the rooms breaks with more traditional housing models. This calls hierarchies into question, and by extension, the distribution of care management or unpaid work, which, associated with inherited gender roles, often underlie them. Likewise, there are no corridors, but an adjacency connected by an enfilade which, in this case, is distorted by a diagonal movement. This enfilade continues to cause tension between the delimited and the continuous, but in this case, they advance on the work of Office KGDVS by dislocating it. In this way, the enfilade further preserves the independence of the room, but at the same time, reveals the full scale of the apartment by giving us a glimpse of the adjoining rooms without completely revealing the core of any.

However, perhaps where a mannerist attitude is most clearly revealed is in the way MAIO set the building within Barcelona's pre-existing *eixample*,[129] accepting the formal and material conflicts this inevitably produced. This attitude is very different, for example, from that taken by Toyo Ito in previous decades, in which he responded to the same problem in Suites Avenue (2009) with a façade system that overlapped like a continuous veil, without acknowledging any contradiction. On the contrary, MAIO's approach accepts the language and scale of the monumental ambition of the *eixample* and its discreet and repetitive fenestration in the upper structure of the building. Despite this acceptance of an already inherited compositional system, their work rejects the aspects that reinforce this monumentality, denying the frontality of key elements such as the staircase,

---

129 The *eixample* in Catalan, or *ensanche*, in Spanish, is the extension of the city of Barcelona planned by Spanish engineer Ildefonso Cerdá in 1860. However, today, when someone refers to the *eixample* as an area of the city they mostly relate to the central part of it, which developed from the 19th century and where the local middle and upper classes dwelled. Provença street, where the project sits, fits this definition, showcasing a wide spectrum of elegant apartment blocks. It is necessary to remark that the eixample itself has also other realities, such as Poble Nou, for instance, that developed as an industrial hub or Sant Martí, close to it, traditionally occupied by the working classes.

and associating others so that they float freely as islands, forcing one to explore and travel through the space in order to understand it. All the exhibitionism in the bourgeois culture of the *eixample*, its solid and recognizable image, which is commonly demonstrated with an ample frontality, is dislocated and distorted to become a landscape of marble and stuccoes that one must pass through in order to discover, thus transforming what was a representation into a living experience. Here again, we find a reformulation of Venturi's "double-functioning", where elements as practical as a lift acquire an unusually expressive presence and become important pieces in the spatial organization.

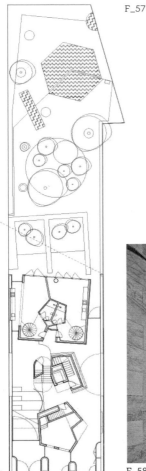

F_57

F_59

F_58

Coda

Many of the firms cited in this book are still in relatively early stages of their careers. Although it remains to be seen whether the formal and material operations they carry out, whether these recurring tensions, dislocations and overlaps, are always the result of a conscious and self-critical attitude towards the very systems in which they work, I like to think that they reveal an attitude that looks with acceptance, but also with optimism, at a situation of continuous crisis. One that accepts the demands of working in an inevitably unstable terrain without trying to dominate it, and without surrendering to it either. The acceptance of this crisis, as seen in these works, does not imply a movement of withdrawal or the need for an architecture of austerity that manifests itself in an elemental or stark aesthetic. Rather, we are faced with a new way of opening up our practice that does not shy away from the intensive development of its own expressive resources in order to reveal itself. This generation's attitude is one that, abandoning the naivety of perfect coherence, reflects the maturity of those who have faced the limitations of small commissions, doubtful clients, economic restrictions or complex starting conditions, and foster a special sensitivity towards what remains on the margins of architecture, always using the tools that architectural practice offers. An attitude unfolds that has a critical capacity, a questioning of the systems that one has inherited as a basis to develop one's work, to enable the architect to incorporate inevitable change that waits at the door: contingencies, programs, contexts, and in a broader sense, issues that are ever-present which are external to the discipline, such as socio-economic, heritage, environmental, biopolitical, gender, public health requirements, the question of identity and even, why not say it, the ultimate incorporation of human subjectivity itself. Perhaps, for this very reason, the attitude referred to is not only something typical of the present moment, but rather a way of accepting an unstable present, which innumerable architects have faced over the course of history.

Bloomsbury, London, 1730. Plan and section. The British Library Archives.

13   Peter Thumb, Pilgrimage Church Birnau, Uhldingen-Muhlhofen, 1747-1750. Photograph by Andreas Praefcke. Wikicommons.

14   Nicholas Hawksmoor, Christ Church in Spitalfields, London, 1729. Photograph by Amanda Slater.

15   Robert Venturi, Beach House, 1959. ©VSBA Archive.

16   Robert Venturi, Beach House, 1959. ©VSBA Archive.

17   Venturi and Short, North Penn Visiting Nurses Association, Lansdale (PA), 1960-1963. Ground floor plan. ©VSBA Archive.

18   Venturi and Short, North Penn Visiting Nurses Association, Lansdale (PA), 1960-1963. Section. ©VSBA Archive.

19   Venturi and Rauch, Vanna Venturi House, Chestnut Hill (PA), 1959-1964. ©VSBA Archive.

20   Venturi and Rauch, Vanna Venturi House, Chestnut Hill (PA), 1959-1964. ©VSBA Archive.

21   Rafael Moneo and Ramón Bescós, Extension of Bankinter Headquarters, Madrid, 1972-76. Axonometric drawing. ©Estudio Rafael Moneo.

22   Alvaro Siza, Banco Pinto & Sotto Mayor, Oliveira de Azeméis, 1971-1974. Plan. ©Alvaro Siza Arquitecto LDA.

23   Lütjens Padmanabhan, Binningen II, Zurich, 2011-2014. Plan. ©Lütjens Padmanabhan

24   Lütjens Padmanabhan, Binningen II, Zurich, 2011-2014. Exterior view. Photograph by Walter Mair. Courtesy of Lütjens Padmanabhan.

25   6a architects, Tree House, London, 2013.

Kersten Geers David Van Severen.

37   OFFICE Kersten Geers David Van Severen, Solo House, Matarraña, 2012-2017. Plan. ©OFFICE Kersten Geers David Van Severen.

38   OFFICE Kersten Geers David Van Severen, Solo House, Matarraña, 2012-2017. Photograph by Bas Princen. Courtesy of OFFICE Kersten Geers David Van Severen.

39   architecten de vylder vinck taillieu, Verzameld Werk Gallery, Ghent, 2001. Photograph by Filip Dujardin. Courtesy of architecten de vylder vinck taillieu/ architecten jan de vylder inge vinck/jo taillieu architecten.

40   architecten de vylder vinck taillieu, Twiggy store, Ghent, 2012. Photograph by Filip Dujardin. Courtesy of architecten de vylder vinck taillieu/ architecten jan de vylder inge vinck/jo taillieu architecten.

41   architecten de vylder vinck taillieu, Scheep Los, undisclosed place in Belgium, 2011. Interior view. Photograph by Filip Dujardin. Courtesy of architecten de vylder vinck taillieu/ architecten jan de vylder inge vinck/jo taillieu architecten.

42   architecten de vylder vinck taillieu, Scheep Los, undisclosed place in Belgium, 2011. Section. ©architecten de vylder vinck taillieu/ architecten jan de vylder inge vinck/jo taillieu architecten.

43   architecten de vylder vinck taillieu, Scheep CG House, undisclosed location in Belgium, 2016-17. Conceptual plan. ©architecten de vylder vinck taillieu/ architecten jan de vylder inge vinck/jo taillieu architecten.

44   architecten de vylder vinck taillieu, Scheep CG House, undisclosed location in Belgium, 2016-17. Photograph by Filip Dujardin. Courtesy of architecten de vylder vinck taillieu/ architecten jan de vylder inge vinck/jo taillieu architecten.

Díaz. Courtesy of Ted'A arquitectes.

54 MAIO, 110 Rooms, Barcelona, 2013-2017. Typical plan. ©MAIO.

55 MAIO, 110 Rooms, Barcelona, 2013-2017. Apartment interior. Photograph by José Hevia. Courtesy of MAIO.

56 TEd'A arquitectes, Can Jaime i n'Isabelle, Palma de Mallorca, 2011-2018. Photographs by Luis Díaz. Courtesy of Ted'A arquitectes.

57 MAIO, 110 Rooms, Barcelona, 2013-2017. Ground floor plan. ©MAIO.

58 MAIO, 110 Rooms, Barcelona, 2013-2017. Entrance hall. Photograph by José Hevia. Courtesy of MAIO..

59 MAIO, 110 Rooms, Barcelona, 2013-2017. Main Façade. Photograph by José Hevia. Courtesy of MAIO.

Bibliography

Agamben, Giorgio. *What is an apparatus? And other essays.* Stanford, CA: Standford University Press, 2009.

architecten de vylder vinck taillieu, *architecten de vylder vinck taillieu.* Ghent: MER, 2011.

Argan, Giulio Carlo. *Storia dell'arte italiana II.* Florence: Sansoni, 1968.

Aureli, Pier Vittorio. *The Possibility of an Absolute Architecture.* New York: The MIT Press, 2011.

Aureli, Pier Vittorio. "Mannerism, or the «Manner» at the Time of Eisenman," in *Peter Eisenman. Barefoot on White-Hot Walls*, ed. Peter Noever, 66–74. Vienna: Hatje Cantz, 2004.

Banham, Reyner. "The new brutalism," *Architectural Review* 118 (December 1955): 354-361.

Baraona Pohl, Ethel. "Smells Like Teen Spirit," *Harvard Design Magazine* 44. (Fall/Winter 2017): 156-161.

Blunt, Anthony. "Mannerism in Architecture," *Journal of the RIBA* 56, serie 3, no. 5 (1949): 195–201.

Borasi, Giovanna, dir. *AP164: Ábalos & Herreros. Selected by Kersten Geers and David Van Severen, Juan José Castellón González, Florian Idenburg and Jing Liu with an interpretation in photographs by Stefano Graziani.* Montreal: Canadian Centre for Architecture; Zurich: Park Books, 2016.

Dvořak, Max. *Kunstgeschichte als Geistesgeschichte.* Munich: Piper, 1924.

Eliot, T. S. *Use of Poetry and Use of Criticism.* Harvard University Press. Cambridge, AM, 1933.

Ernst Robert Curtius, *European literature and the Latin Middle Ages* (New York: Princeton University Press, 2013

Foucault, Michel: "Panopticism", in *Discipline & Punish: The Birth of the Prison.* New York: Vintage Books, 1977, 195-228.

Friedlaender, Walter. *Mannerism and Anti-Matterism in Italian Painting*. New York: Columbia University Press, 1957.

Geers, Kersten and Van Severen, David. "Solo House, Matarraña (Teruel), 2012-2017," *Quaderns d'arquitectura i urbanisme* 270 (2018): 37-43.

Geers, Kersten, Pančevac, Jelena, and Zanderigo, Andrea, eds. *The Difficult Whole: A Reference Book on Robert Venturi, John Rauch and Denise Scott Brown*. Houston: Park Books, 2016.

Geers, Kersten. "Architecture without Content," *Harvard design magazine* 43 (October 2016): 108-110

Geers, Kersten et al. *Architecture Without Content*. London: Bedford Press, 2015.

Geers, Kersten. "Siza's Mother," *San Rocco* 7 (2013): 18-22.

González de Canales, Francisco. "Subjetivar la máquina. La casa Gordillo de Ábalos & Herreros," in *Arquitectura española y tecnología*. Sevilla: Recolectores Urbanos, 2020.

González de Canales, Francisco. "Politics of the domestic," in *José Ramón Sierra 2015*. Sevilla: Recolectores Urbanos, 78-105.

González de Canales, Francisco, and Ray, Nicholas. "Rafael Moneo and the search for a reflexive canon of knowledge," *The Journal of Architecture* 19, no.5 (2014): 693-722.

González de Canales, Francisco. "A stay outside", in *Experiments with life itself*. Barcelona: Actar, 2012.

Hauser, Arnold. *Mannerism: the crisis of the Renaissance and the origin of Modern Art*. Cambridge, MA: Belknap Press of Harvard University Press, 1986 (first published in 1965).

Hejduk, John. *Mask of Medusa*. New York: Rizzoli, 1985.

Bibliography

Hocke, Gustav René. *Die Welt als Labyrinth. Manier und Manie in der europäischen Kunst. Beiträge zur Ikonographie und Formgeschichte der europäischen Kunst von 1520 bis 1650 und der Gegenwart.* Hamburg: Rowohlt, 1957.

Jeffries, Stuart. *Grand Hotel Abyss: The Lives of the Frankfurt School.* London: Verso, 2016.

Kepes, Gyorgy. *Language of vision.* Chicago: Theobold, 1944.

Koolhaas, Rem. "Bigness or the problem of Large Rem Koolhaas," in *Small, Medium, Large, Extra-Large.* New York: Monacelli Press, 1995, 506-508.

Leach, Andrew. *Crisis on Crisis.* Basel: Standpunkte, 2017.

Lévi-Strauss, Claude. *The Savage Mind.* London: Weidenfeld and Nicolson, 1964.

Lotz, Wolfgang. *Architecture in Italy, 1500-1600.* London: Penguin Books, 1974.

Márquez Cecilia, Fernando, and Levene, Richard eds. *6a architects 2009-2017: adjustments.* El Croquis 192. Madrid: El Croquis, 2017.

Márquez Cecilia, Fernando, and Levene, Richard eds. *Office Kerstan Geers David van Severen: primary actions, 2003-2016.* El Croquis 185. Madrid: El Croquis, 2016.

Márquez Cecilia, Fernando, and Levene, Richard eds. *TEd'A arquitectes 2010-018: material in play.* El Croquis 196. Madrid: El Croquis, 2018.

Maxwell, Robert. "Situating Stirling," *Architectural Review* 1370 (April 2011): 72-81

Morin, Edgard. *On Complexity.* New York, Hampton Press, 2008.

Morin, Edgard. "The Need for Complex Thought," *Sociétés* (November 1998): 57-62.

Morin, Edgard. "Pour une crisologie," *Communications* 25 (1976): 149-163.

Padmanabhan, Thomas, and Lütjens, Oliver, "Venturi's First," *San Rocco* 4, (2010): 112- 115; "A day at the beach" *in San Rocco* 14 (2018): 206-209

Panofsky, Erwin. *Idea. A Contribution to Art Theory.* Columbia: University of South Carolina Press, 1968.

Panofsky, Erwin. *Gothic architecture and scholasticism.* New York: Meridian Books, 1957-

Pevsner, Nikolaus. *The Architecture of Mannerism.* Londres: Routledge, 1946.

Puente, Moisés, and Puyuelo, Anna, eds. architecten de vylder vinck taillieu. 2G 66. Barcelona: Gustavo Gili, 2013.

Puente, Moisés, and Puyuelo, Anna, eds. *OFFICE Kersten Gers David van Severen.* 2G 63. Barcelona: Gustavo Gili, 2012.

Quintans, Carlos. *architecten de vylder vinck taillieu, Archives* 3. Barcelona: Polígrafa, 2018.

Richter, Melvin, and Richter, Michaela W. "Translation of Reinhart Koselleck's Krise, in Geschichtliche Grundbegriffe," *Journal of the History of Ideas* 67, no. 2 (April 2006): 343-356; translated from, Otto Brunner, Werner Konze, and Reinhart Koselleck, eds. *Geschichtliche Grundbegriffe: Historisches Lexicon zur politisch-sozialen Sprache in Deutschland,* 8 volumes (Stuttgart: Klett-Cotta, 1972-97).

Rousselot, Christine, and Beaudouin, Laurent. "Entretien avec Alvaro Siza," *AMC* 44 (February, 1978): 36.

Rowe, Colin, and Koetter, Fred. *Collage City.* Cambridge, MA: The MIT Press, 1978.

Rowe, Colin. "Introduction", in *Five Architects. Eisenman, Graves, Gwathmey, Hejduk, Meier.* New York: Oxford University Press, 1975, 3-7.

Rowe, Colin. "Mannerism and Modern Architecture," *Architectural Review* 107 (March 1950): 289–299.

Bibliography

Rowe, Colin. "Mathematics of the Ideal Villa: Palladio and Le Corbusier compared," *Architectural Review* 101 (March 1947): 101-4.

Scalbert, Irénée and 6a architects, *Never Modern*. Zurich: Park Books, 2013.

Scott Brown, Denise and Venturi, Robert. Architecture as *Signs and Systems for a Mannerist Time*. Cambridge: Harvard University Press, 2004.

Scott Brown, Denise, and Robert Venturi. *A View from the Campidoglio: Selected Essays 1953-1984*. New York: Harper and Row, 1984.

Scott Brown, Denise, Venturi, Robert and Izenour, Steven. *Learning from Las Vegas*. Cambridge, MA: MIT Press, 1978.

Shearman, John. *Mannerism*. London: Penguin books, 1967.

Sloterdijk, Peter. "Rules for the Human Zoo: a response to the Letter on Humanism," *Environment and Planning D: Society and Space* 27 (2009): 12-28.

Smithson, Alison and Peter. "The «As Found» and the «Found,»" in David Robbins, ed. *The Independent Group: Postwar Britain and the Aesthetics of Plenty*. London and Cambridge, MA: The MIT Press, 1990, 201-202.

Smyth, Craig Hugh. Mannerism and Maniera. New York: J. J. Augustin for The Institute of Fine Arts, New York University, 1962.

Stierli, Martino, and Brownlee, David B., eds. Complexity and Contradiction at Fifty. New York: MOMA, 2019.

Stierli, Martino. "In the Academy's Garden: Robert Venturi, the Grand Tour and the Revision of Modern Architecture," AA Files 56 (2007): 42-56.

Tafuri, Manfredo. *Retórica y experimentalismo. Ensayos sobre la arquitectura de los siglos XVI y XVII*. Seville: Universidad de Sevilla, 1978.

Tafuri, Manfredo. "Design and techno utopia" in Emilio Ambasz, ed. *Italy, the new domestic landscape: achievements and problems of Italian design.* New York: Museum of Modern Art, 1972, 388-404.

Tafuri, Manfredo. *L'architettura del manierismo nel Cinquecento europeo.* Rome: Officina de Architettura, 1966.

Vasari, Giorgio. *The lives of the most excellent painters, sculptors, and architects.* New York: Modern Library, 2006 (first published as a revised edition of the book in 1568).

Venturi, Robert. "Viva Mannerism for an architecture for our age", *Log* 13 (2008): 52-53.

Venturi, Robert and Rossi, Aldo. Mother's House. *The evolution of Vanna Venturi's House in Chesnut Hill.* New York: Rizzoli, 1992.

Venturi, Robert. *Complexity and Contradiction in Architecture.* New York: MoMA, 1965.

Venturi, Robert. "A Justification for a Pop Architecture," *Arts and Architecture* 82, no. 4 (April 1965): 22.

Venturi, Robert. "The Campidoglio: A Case Study," *Architectural Review* 113, no. 32 (May 1953): 333–34.

Vidotto, Marco: *Alison + Peter Smithson. Works & Projects.* Barcelona and New York: Whitney Library of Design and GG, 1997.

Wilson, Rob. "Fivefold," *Architectural Review* 1412 (October 2014): 56-69.

Wittkower, Rudolf. *Architectural Principles in the Age of Humanism.* London: The Warburg Institute, 1949.

Wittkower, Rudolf. "Principle's of Palladio's Architecture," *Journal of the Warburg and Courtauld Institutes*, vol. 7 (1944): 102-122.

Acknowledgements

107 In many everyday conversations with colleagues, presentations to symposia and students, and informal talks, I have continuously discussed many of the aspects that built up to this book. For me, this is a very personal work, but at the same time, a very collective one. It is for this reason that it is difficult to delimit a realm of thanks. However, there are certain individuals that had a clear impact on the final outcome of this book, and I would like to highlight them.

I would really like to thank Ingrid Schroder and the Architectural Association for their support in the publication of this book. I would really like to thank as well, the introductory words written by Rafael Moneo, but also his comments on the manuscript long before. I need to thank Denise Scott Brown for helping me frame the context for some relevant elements of the book, and for giving me valuable advice to make it a better one. I am also indebted to Enrique Walker who offered very relevant points to my first manuscript. I also need to highlight the remarks to the text offered by Eduardo Prieto, with whom I am still in debt. I would like to thank Jacobo García-German as well: this book is an extension of our collaboration for A Minor Architecture exhibition, and everything that came after that. I really need to thank Paula Álvarez, who played a fundamental role in a previous version of this book in Spanish. And of course, I am always indebted to my closer intellectual partner, Nuria Álvarez Lombardero, who always offers relevant insights into everything I do in life.

I would also like to thank the work of Vincent Morales, Megan Connolly and Aram Mooradian on the English edition of the text. I am grateful to the work of Ricardo Devesa for his editorial work on the book and to the elegant design by Camila Joaqui and the final adjusements by Sofia Sandoval. The book would not have been possible

108 without the generosity of the practices whose materials are published in this book: Venturi Scott Brown and Associates, Rafael Moneo, Alvaro Siza, Lütjens Padmanabhan, 6a architects, Office Kersten Geer David Van Severen, architekten de vylder vinck taillieu, TEd'A arquitectes and Maio architects.

Finally, I would also like to extend my gratitude to all the colleagues with whom I have been able to hold conversations at some point on topics that could concern the discussion of this book. In alphabetical order, and I hope that I could be forgiven me for those I couldn't remember: Ana Araujo, Pier Vittorio Aureli, Anna Bach, Eugeni Bach, Isabelle Blancke, Fabrizio Ballabio, Shumi Bose, Matilde Cassani, Álvaro Carrillo Eguilaz, Javier Castellano Pulido, Silvia Colmenares, Manuel Collado, Ryan Dillon, Tom Emerson, Guillermo Fernández-Abascal, Pascal Flammer, Eva Franch i Gilabert, Aitor Fuentes, Carolina García Estévez, Tomás García Píriz, Kersten Geers, José Gómez Mora, María González, Wiston Hampel, Diego Jiménez, Max Khalen, Kostandis Kizis, Lara Lesmes, Guillermo López, Juanjo López de la Cruz, Oliver Lütjens, Taneli Mansikkamäki, Ángel Martínez García-Posada, Jaume Mayol, Pedro Mena, Toni Moll, Daniel Montes, Joaquim Moreno, Hikaru Nissanke, Marta Pelegrín, Moisés Puente, Jessica Reynolds, Luis Rojo, Pablo Ros, Borja Sallago, José María Sánchez, Giles Smith, Javier Terrados, Max Turnheim and Jan de Vylder.

The Mannerist Mind
An Architecture of Crisis

Published by
Actar Publishers
New York / Barcelona
www.actar.com

Authors
English version by Vincent Morales, Aram Mooradian and Francisco González de Canales

Editorial Design
Actar, María Camila Joaqui

Printed in Spain

Publication date
June 2023

ISBN: 978-1-63840-036-3
LCCN: 2022942871

A CIP catalogue record for this book is available from the Library of Congress, Washington, DC, USA.

Distributed by
Actar D, Inc.

New York
440 Park Avenue South, 17 Fl.
New York, NY 10016, USA
+12129662207
salesnewyork@actar-d.com

Barcelona
Roca i Batlle, 2-4
08023 Barcelona, Spain
+34 933 282 183
eurosales@actar-d.com

Design and authorship:
The Manerist Mind

Cover design:
Marga Gibert Valls

Part of this work was first presented in Spanish as El Manierismo y su Ahora. Una Aproximación Optimista para un Presente Incierto. Sevilla: Vibok Works, 2022.

With the support of the Architectural Association, London